Easy Reading Writing

Novels by Peter E. Abresch

Bloody Bonsai

Killing Thyme

Tip A Canoe

Peter@elderhostelmysteries.com
http://www.easyreadingwriting.com/

Easy Reading Writing

by

Peter E. Abresch

Easy Reading about Writing Easy Reading

Published in the United States of America by:

Scrivenery Press
P.O. Box 740969-1003
Houston, TX 77274-0969
www.scrivenery.com

First Edition

Cover by Françoise Merot, based on artwork by Lisa Zador, New York (www.lisazador.com). Interior illustrations by Norman Schureman.

The book block is digitally typeset in Minion *and* Minion Expert, *by Adobe Systems Incorporated (www.adobe.com).*

01 02 03 SP 10 9 8 7 6 5 4 3 2 1

Library of Congress Cataloging-in-Publication Data

Abresch, Peter E.
Easy reading writing : easy reading about writing easy reading / by Peter E. Abresch.--1st ed.
p. cm.
ISBN 1-893818-05-5 (alk. paper)
1. Fiction--Authorship. 2. High interest-low vocabulary books. I. Title.

PN3355 .A27 2001
808.3--dc21

2001034491

for

Dorrie (Dodee) O'Brien

nothing happened *till* you took a chance on me

Acknowledgments

Marcie Heidish, David Hoff
who set me on the right path

Dewey Pleake who read the manual

Ed Williams and Kevin Miller
for the great editing job at Scrivenery Press

For those who used to hang out at
Harry's (virtual) Bar and Grill

Susan, Tonyia, Patrice, 'Bama, Bruce, BVD Jenn, Spinner
Beth Amos, Doug Clegg, Larry Crews
Jim Cypher, Digby Diehl, David Feldman
Susan Henry, Bert Latimore, Cyn Mobley
Tom Orem, Ed Wyrick
all the others lost in the crash of my mind's hard drive
and, in memory
Harry Arnston

I wouldn't have made it without you guys

also to

J. Alcc West
Alec@NovelHost.net
who helped me set up my Web page
http://www.easyreadingwriting.com/

Your purchase of Easy Reading Writing entitles you to receive free updates via an e-mail newsletter. To subscribe, send a blank e-mail with the word "subscribe" (without quotation marks) in the subject line to:

ERWnewsletter-request@ElderhostelMysteries.com

You can also visit with Peter Abresch at the message board called the Locutory, on the Scrivenery Press Web site:

http://www.scrivenery.com/

Easy reading is damn hard writing.

—Nathaniel Hawthorne

or Maya Angelou
or Robert Louis Stevenson
or Robert Seeley
or Robert Burns
or William Zinsser
or...

Table of Contents

When you first start to write you get all the kick and the reader gets none, but after you learn to work it's your object to convey everything to the reader so that he remembers it not as a story he had read but something that happened to himself. That's the true test of writing. When you can do that, the reader gets the kick and you don't get any. You just get hard work and the better you write the harder it is because every story has to be better than the last one. It's the hardest work there is.

—Ernest Hemingway

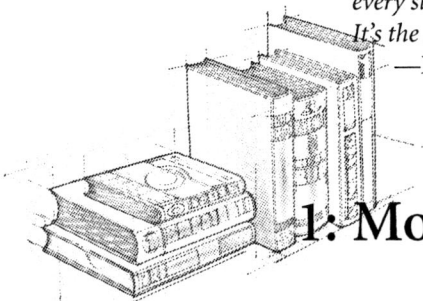

1: Motivation

Easy reading is damn hard writing.

I haven't been able to pin down exactly who said that, but I'm here to attest to its veracity. If we want to write so that readers will pick up our work, become submerged in it, move into our story like they are watching a movie—better still, like they are living it—then that requires damn hard work.

So if you're looking for an easy way to fame and fortune, you might want to consider placing this back on the shelf and tiptoeing away.

Also, it takes some knowledge to write easy reading.

Just because we can walk eight miles doesn't mean we are ready to hike up Mount Everest. To reach the summit we'd have to learn climbing techniques, where to drive pitons, how to cling to rock faces.

What we'd need is a Sherpa guide.

So it is with writing. Just because we can pen letters and memos doesn't mean we can write a novel. This requires a special knowledge of building characters, working out logical plots, handling believable dialogue—all learnable but necessary skills.

That's what this book is about.

It's a Sherpa guide up the rock face of Plot-line Mountain.

The problem with books on writing is that they are often difficult to read. Does that sound right? Good writing should be easy to read. If we are trying to teach easy-reading writing, shouldn't our books on writing be easy reading? Or at least interesting reading?

Leaf through this book. If you are having trouble reading it, hey, toss it onto the shelf. It probably means I don't know what I'm talking about.

There are also some dangers lurking here.

Fiction writing is addictive.

You laugh, but once I started building worlds on paper I found there was always a force calling me back. It didn't make any difference how many failures I had, how many rejection slips I collected—more than my share—how many times I smashed up typewriters or suffered through hard drive crashes, I could never turn off that seductive siren call that still wafts across the water on my brain, whispering how *big* my next novel will be. Oh, yeah.

So unless you're serious about stringing words together, jam this book back in the stack.

Fiction writing is also coolie labor. I'm on my computer first thing in the morning and many times I'm still there, with breaks for food and naps, till nine or ten at night. This for a salary that would turn away day workers in Bangladesh.

So if your thought is to pop out a few fast mysteries and make some easy bucks, well, do I still have to tell you what to do with this book?

Writing is like painting, or playing an oboe, or maybe even like basketball. If you want to be good at it, you practice everyday, often not knowing whether you're getting better or worse. And it isn't about success. Of all those out there trying, how many actually make it to the NBA? Or play oboe in a major orchestra? Writing is a hunger not dependent on money or admiration. And not so much on talent, folks. Talent is cheap. It's persistence that wins the day, the dogged struggle to be better, to find another way of conveying feeling, joy and sorrow, light and darkness, of colors playing in the shadows. In the end, it's the struggle that becomes the mission. And I keep at it because, when it's right, those rare moments when it's on, and an idea or a phrase comes drifting out of the ether so startling I have to say, "Wow, where did that come from," and I know it's a keeper; it's like being touched by God.

This book is an expedition through the briars and brambles that link those rare moments together. It will not guarantee that you will make big bucks, or even be published by a non-fee press. I would be less than honest if I didn't tell you, contrary to what is splashed across magazines and book covers, the odds are stacked against that. What this journey will do is give you the tools to help you become the best writer you can be, to solve some of the problems of which Hemingway said, "We are all apprentices in a craft where no one ever becomes a master."

If you feel like it, climb aboard.

There's talent and there's potential. Potential is what you make of your talent.

—Lance Armstrong, two-time winner of the Tour de France

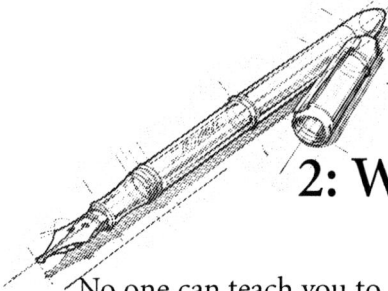

2: Welcome Aboard

No one can teach you to write fiction.

Say what?

Then why did I buy this book?

Because we can point out the elements that are necessary to go into good fiction. Like drawing characters that live and breathe in our readers' minds. Plots that unfold like a movie in our readers' minds. Dialogue that rings as true as the spoken words in our readers' minds.

That's the fiction writer's field of play.

We're not in the business of *telling* stories.

We're in the business of building images in our readers' minds and bundling them together to *show* a story.

When you stop to think about it, that's probably the whole reason language was invented in the first place.

For essentials man could always get by with an odd word here or there.

Bread. Water. Meat. Sex. Headache.

Ah, but when he came back to his cave and wanted tell his woman and children the story of the hunt, it required taking the pictures in the storyteller's mind and building them in the listener's mind. To do that he not only had to evoke images of things the listener knew, but also of things the listener had never imagined. To do that, he had to string words together. And to do that, he needed language.

> He stood on a ribbon of sand stretched taut between leaden horizons and walled in by a somber sea on one side, faceless dunes on the other. A lone gull scudded by on the gelid salt air with only its plaintive cry to break the solitude of wind and waves.

What senses do we touch upon here? Sight, of course. Salt air recalls the smell of a beach and perhaps the taste of it upon our lips. There's sound in the gull's call and in the wind and waves. The gelid air reminds us of the feel of a cold wind upon our skin. That's all five senses. But we also use words that play on our emotions: *lone* gull; *faceless* dunes; the *solitude* of wind and waves. All these combine to give us the feeling of isolation. *Walled in* by a *somber* sea, the dunes, and *leaden* horizons gives the feeling of being boxed in. Finally, he stood on a ribbon *stretched taut*, as if something is about to snap.

Our job is not to tell our story; our job is to choose words that will start the movie projector rolling in our readers' minds, words that coax out sensory memories—see, taste, touch, smell, hear—to trigger our readers' imagination and life experiences. If we could take a snapshot of the image the above description evokes in the minds of a hundred people, they would all be different, depending on their individual environments, education, backgrounds, and DNA.

Do we care?

Not a whit.

What's important is that our readers create their version of our world inside their heads, because when they do that, it plops them right in the middle of the action, and they experience the story taking place around them.

That's what our job is.

It's not easy.

Easy reading is hard writing.

There are no books, formulas or computer programs that will insure success. If there were, we'd all be using them.

We can point out the direction to the mountaintop, but each of us has to make the journey on our own. And none of us will take the same path.

I've read books on writing that say to be successful you must build your characters first, that you work out your plot first, that you must start out with an outline, that you must not start out with an outline.

Fagetaboutit.

We all have individual memories, imaginations, life experiences, word prints, DNA. Each guitarist has a different strum. Each painter a different brush stroke. Even each telegraph operator has a different fist, the way they key dots and dashes. Just so each writer. Only by working at it can we learn to develop our own unique style, our own unique way of stringing words together, the unique characters and unique stories that reside only in our unique heads. Only by writing and rewriting can we develop a smoothness that leads one sentence into another, one paragraph to another, and one chapter into another. These can only come about by connecting our mind to our fingers and doing it over and over again.

The Writing Tripod

Even so, it takes three things, like the legs of a tripod, for a story to stand.

Plot. Characterization. Effective writing.

Yes, we can talk about other things like dialogue and description, but these slip under more than one heading. Good dialogue not only comes under effective writing, but is also a feature of good characterization. Description's not only part of a good plot, it is a feature of characterization, letting us see both the picture and the one who sees it. If the writing's effective, it will also convey mood.

Plot. Characterization. Effective writing.

If we forget about any one of these tripod legs, the whole structure comes crumbling down. We might put more emphasis on one, such as a literary work might be read for the pure joy of the way words are strung together, but if we eliminate plot, it goes nowhere and we have no story. If we drop characterization, we can have a good story line and effective writing, but people that nobody cares about. Good plot and good characters, but poor writing, who will bother to plow through it?

A fantastic plot might occasionally get by with cardboard characters, and yes, some genres pay less attention to characterization, but how much better if we people this fantastic plot with characters our readers can identify with and care about?

On the other hand, a character story will suffer if it doesn't have conflict and suspense to drive it. Then there's effective writing.

Effective writing, folks, is rewriting. It's reworking everything until it is sparse, crystal clear, conveying mood and sight and feel and taste and sound, using no more words than are absolutely necessary, squeezing out the fat to leave a rich, simmering broth. It is the soup that binds the flavors of plot and characterization as surely as that of chicken and garlic.

In these days of shrinking budgets, it is important for us to give publishers a story that refuses to be put down. If we are strong in one category, we have to study and work on the other two to bring them in balance.

But we know big name authors with cardboard characters, right? And poor writing? And dumb plots? How come big names get away with slop?

Agent Joshua Bilmes of the Jabberwocky Literary Agency put it this way. "When an author comes to an agent he is selling two things, his sales history and his book. The more you have of one, the less you need of the other."

Since we have none of the former, we need all of the latter.

I'm telling you all this because I wish I had known it thirty-five years ago. I believe I've always had good plots, but I had no idea about characterization. I had no one to sit me down and point out why my hero was a stick figure, or how to make my sentences flow. That's what we're trying to do on this writing adventure.

If all this sounds daunting, folks, remember we don't have to get it right the first time.

Relax.

Consider the work of a potter.

Anybody can roll clay into long ropes, stack them into a vessel, and fire it into a pot that will hold water.

But if you want an elegant vase that is not only utilitarian, but is pleasing to the eye as well, you have to turn it on a wheel, work it under your fingers, shape it, reshape it, maybe punching it down to start again. And again. Only the fingers and eyes can tell when it's right. The more you do it doesn't mean it will get any easier, but the practice will more perfectly transform the image of the mind into the mud in the hands until, one day, it passes from the stage of clay pot into the realm of fine art.

That's the secret of fiction writing, folks.

Not being afraid to write something badly.

And then sitting down alone at the wheel and turning the jumble of words into a thing of art.

The world needs its storytellers. Do what you need to do to allow that gift to grow.
—Kathy Thirtyacre

3: Getting Started

When writing about writing, it's tricky to figure what order to introduce each subject. There's so much to learn. It's too bad I can't do a digital dump to your brain, like getting a wave of light in one full swoop rather than parceling out the rainbow one color at a time.

I chose this order with the newest tenderfoot in mind, anxious to begin pounding away on a keyboard and squeezing in time to read this book while commuting, babysitting, or making strange noises in the john. While the well-traveled yarn-masters may be tempted to mosey down the trail, they may miss something basic they overlooked the first time through.

Caveat

First there's a couple of cautions.

If you have a finished manuscript and are considering submitting it, you need to take a look at chapters twenty-eight through thirty: *Beware*, lest you place your money on a one way ride to Indiana Jones's lost temple of doom; *After the Last Draft*, lest you prejudice your manuscript before it's even read; and *Where Do We Send It*, lest your hard-toiled work bask forever in a watery grave.

Now we're ready to board the boat upriver.

Create on a Computer

Create on a computer?

This is some pearl of wisdom?

This is a pearl of wisdom.

For the beginner, I urge you to do everything on the computer right from the start. Time spent in a learning curve now will pay big dividends. Printed words look different than written words. What looked good in longhand will often look not-good in print. Besides, everything will have to be keyboarded in eventually, probably introducing errors and head scratching.

Okay, some people can't work on a computer.

I have a friend, Marcy Heidish, who I think has a computer phobia and uses a battered old typewriter for creating and rewriting, but she has eight published novels. My Internet friend, Cyndy Mobley, creates by voice, using a speech conversion program which translates it into printed words on the computer, and she has published a passel of books in a short time. Then there's Elmore Leonard who creates and rewrites longhand, using lined yellow paper he has specially made for him, and gives the final to his daughter to type. I've heard he has one or two books out. Oh, yeah.

So, whatever works, works.

But it's so much easier if you can go from start to finish using the computer.

And if you can't create on a computer, try rewriting on it. With a computer it's easy to shift words, sentences, and paragraphs for greater effect and smoothness. We can recopy a troubling section and work on it, see how it holds together, rework it again, and compare it with the original. When we're happy with it, it's a simple matter of plugging it back into the page and checking out how it looks in relation to the paragraphs before and after it.

When I started writing, in the dark age of typewriters, I decided to write each paragraph at least three times to keep from being tempted to say it was good enough. The original when I went through the first draft. Then I'd copy it onto a second sheet of paper where I would retype it until I was satisfied, and then add it to the final draft. This practice kept me from concentrating only on a difficult word or sentence, but rather how it all fit together. Since I forced myself to retype the whole paragraph, I would experiment with the order of the sentences, consolidating thought patterns so it flowed logically. Then I checked to see how the paragraph fit into the page.

All of these things are necessary if we are to eliminate reusing words, redundancy, and jumbled thought. Even so, when I found something not quite right in the finished product, I would occasionally accept it rather than ask my wife to retype the page.

But this is all sliced bread on a computer.

Of course, we can do it all with pencil or pen as well, but it's a lot more work to recopy a whole paragraph by long hand, changing a few sentences or words as we go. Then will we do it again if it's not quite right? Or will we plug in words here and there and accept it as good enough?

Big name authors can get away with slop.

For you and I to get published we better turn in the absolute best writing we can.

There's also a caveat for writing on a computer.

Can you say, backup?

Do it every day onto a separate disk. And use different disks for different drafts. Make it a religion. If you lose your hard drive, you don't want to lose months or years of work.

When a typewriter goes down, it goes piecemeal.

Once during a super lean time in my life, my "Q" key quit. I kept on writing, substituting the "+" key for the "Q". It looked strange, but it got me by. Then the "?" key started sticking in the key guide and I had to reach up and pull it back. But I kept going, automatically reaching up to pull pack the "?" and hitting the "+" for a "Q". Then one day I looked up to see I had been retyping the same line over and over and over again. When I hit the return bar the platen failed to advance.

I picked up the typewriter and threw it down on the floor. Picked it up and crashed it down it again. Then raised it over my head and smashed it down again, bouncing it two or three times. When I looked up my wide-eyed wife was staring at me from the doorway.

I said, "I need a new typewriter."

She didn't argue.

When I lost my computer's hard drive, it was, to use a cliché, in a blink of an eye. Totally here, totally gone.

I calmly raised my face and said to the heavens, "*Shit.*"

But I didn't lose any work.

What Should We Write About?

There's a pair of questions that always come up at writers' conferences, asked by those first starting out. If you've been on this journey awhile you might want to skip them.

The first, what should I write about?

And immediately someone will pipe up with the cliché, "Write about what you know."

The thing is, suppose you're a plumber. Nothing wrong with that; it's an honorable and well-paid profession. But if you hate doing it, do you think you'll generate much excitement writing about it?

On the other hand, there are a lot of good novels out about the Civil War. *Cold Mountain* by Charles Frazier comes to mind.

I doubt if any of these authors served in that war or lived during those times, but I bet they all were interested in it, researched it, and wrote about it because it excited them.

So I think we should write about what excites us; that excitement will transfer onto the page. It will mean more work and more research, but because it interests us we'll stick with it when the going gets tough.

The other question is, what are publishers looking for?

That's not a bad question. If we can cut across the grass rather than taking the long road around the park, wouldn't we do it?

The problem is, even if we knew what publishers are looking for today, who knows what they will be looking for by the time we get the story written? And even if we knew what they will be looking for then, we're back to the problem of writing about plumbing. We'll be trying to write something that interests someone else rather than what excites us. This works for non-fiction when it is mainly doing the research, gathering facts, and writing it up. Fiction is all that plus reaching down into ourselves and creating an imaginary world.

We can't write someone else's story.

We have to go with an idea that excites us enough to ram thought through our fingers to paint our world in words. And if we do it well enough, that will be the story publishers will be looking for.

The Idea

Okay, we need an idea. Again, this is something more experienced writers might want to slide around.

Ideas are cheap. Ideas cannot be copyrighted. Almost everyone thinks they have a great idea for a novel that's completely different from anything that's ever been done before. In fact, two different people have offered me their great ideas with the comment that *all* I had to do is write it up for a sure-fire bestseller and we split the profits.

Oh, yeah.

There only exist twenty basic plots that have been done over and over again since man first started telling stories. What makes them unique is what we bring to the table.

Our idea can be for a plot. Suppose a man awakens to find himself in a strange airport? In a different time? What would he do? What would happen next? And after that?

Or it can be for a character, say, Sundance Moonflower. What is she like? Chances are with a name like that she's a Native American or a sci-fi person. How does that affect her? Where does she live? What does she want? How is she going to go about getting it?

That's how a story idea develops. Asking questions.

Who, what, where, when, why, and how.

Then finding the answers. Figure out the "who, what, where, when, and how" and we'll have our story.

Sometimes a single event will spark an idea that I'll carry around for months, years in one case, before the rest of the story clicks into place. At other times I'll pop up early in the morning, like God speaking to me—wow, wouldn't it be neat to try this? I know of one woman who must have a title before she can begin. Others keep meticulous notes on various subjects of interest, and keep adding to them, and when one reaches critical mass, they go to work.

Just remember that everyone works differently. If our mind is geared to building characters and we develop them first, we'll still need a plot to make them work. If we're geared to building plots, we'll have to develop our characters as we go along. We need both plot and characters, but which we develop first depends on which turns us on and gets the creative juices flowing.

Building the Story

So we got the idea.

How do we go about putting it together?

Think of fiction writing in terms of scenes. Like the movie we're trying to project in our readers' minds. All the action takes place within these scenes. The scene opens, events take place, the scene closes. This doesn't mean it has to be static; it can be a chase scene with cars careening all over the place. Nor do they need be in sequential order. Breaking everything down into scenes allows us to think of the story in bite-sized portions rather than trying to cram the whole thing into our heads in one swallow. We may relate a scene to a chapter, but a chapter could have more than one scene and a scene could overlap chapters.

Keep a Journal

It's a good idea to keep a journal. Our subconscious feeds us ideas at weird moments and if we copy them down we'll have them to use later. If not, we'll forget. Lots of times I'll wake up with an idea and rather than get up and make a note, I'll snuggle back under the covers repeating a key phrase to myself so I'll remember when I do get up. And I never remember. Now I keep a pad by my bed.

We can jot down thoughts and phrases, pieces of conversation, especially odd words and speech patterns that reflect people's characters and origins. The way people dress. I was on a cruise once and saw a woman in a wheel chair who had a wristwatch on each ankle. I never found out why, but I used that piece of business on a character in *Killing Thyme.*

But I should also tell you, like anything else, whether you keep a journal or not is an individual thing.

Easy Reading

If we want to write easy reading, we have to read books that are easy reading. Read all the time. When I'm not writing, I'm reading, either with a book in my hand, or an audio in my ears. I won't drive to town, mow the lawn, or exercise unless I have a cassette playing. In fact, it got so bad that I've added a daily walk to my exercise routine, deliberately not a taking a cassette player so I can have some quiet time.

I'm a slow reader so I only read about sixty books a year. My friend, Howard Chaykin of comic book fame, reads six books a week. Ugh.

So choose the genre you're interested in writing, and read for pleasure, and read to see how they do it.

Alice K. Turner, fiction editor of *Playboy*, says, "Unless you learn to read intelligently and analytically, you don't have a prayer." Author Steven Spruill, at a Washington Independent Writer's conference, advised that when you are reading as a writer, if you find yourself carried away, stop and figure out what makes it interesting, and if you find yourself bored, stop and figure out why.

A lot of writing teachers advise you to start reading the classics, maybe works of Faulkner and O'Neill. Not me. I'm not saying they don't have a lot to teach us, but they were written for a different age, when people expected a long lead-in to a novel, when they traveled to Europe by ship, and the only satellite in the sky was something called the moon.

Television and movies have changed the perception of how we view stories. We demand to be plugged in by at least the first three pages, better yet, the first three paragraphs. If you want to write easy reading for today's readers, read books that have been written in the last thirty years, better yet, in the last three.

Discipline

People find the time to write in all different ways. Some do it commuting on trains. Others during nap time for the baby. I used to get up at four in the morning to write for a couple of hours while I was fresh before I went to my day job. I got that idea from reading about others who tried it. The thing is, if we are really serious about writing, we have to squeeze in dedicated time somewhere.

It's also better if we can set the same time aside each day, and even the same place. We are creatures of habit. If we can, we'll eat lunch at the same time and at the same cafeteria table, and our mouths will start salivating when we do. So it is with our writing. When the same time and place comes together, the creative part of our brain will be more ready to engage.

This takes understanding from those whose lives it impacts, and it takes discipline from ourselves. We may feel like skipping a day when the going gets tough, but one day can slip to two, and three, and what was initially difficult will continue to grow as the days slip by and the chances increase that we'll never get back to it.

In fact, it's a good idea to quit writing for the day when we're in the middle of something that's moving. We'll be much more anxious to get back than if we are facing a problem that sits there like a fat toad waiting to be kissed.

But, either way, we have to discipline ourselves to keep coming back to the table or we'll never work it through. This is often why a more talented person falls by the wayside while the one with perseverance wins the day. Remember the Tortoise and the Hare? We have to have a hunger for it.

Talent is cheap.

Tenacity is expensive.

Focus on the objective rather than the obstacles.

—Anonymous

4: Preliminaries

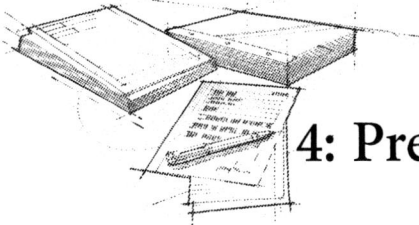

Some of us won't bother with preliminaries. We'll get a story idea into our heads and *charge.* I think Lawrence Block and Barbara D'Amato work this way. So do a lot of mystery writers I know. Their idea is if they work out the plot as they go along, the ending will be a surprise both to themselves and their readers. Some writers also believe that outlining takes the freshness out of their writing, leaving only discouraging drudge labor. Of course, this means hacking our way through the jungle with only a vague idea where the mountain is. For the outliners who wonder how this can be done, there is a great quotation attributed to E.L. Doctorow:

> Writing a novel is like driving a car at night. You can only see as far as your headlights, but you can make the whole trip that way.

Still, we ought to at least check out the preliminaries—outlines, brainstorming, and the most important tool I use, free association—before we go charging off into the bush. Even if we don't use them now, the knowledge could help us out of a stuck spot sometime in the future.

Outlines

Outlines are like sex. Some people like a lot of foreplay; others like to get right at it.

Maybe that's not a good analogy.

While some writers think outlines take the fun out of writing, others look forward to completing their outline so they can then get down to the exciting part. For them an outline is a skeleton about which to build up flesh and muscles and sinews and all the fun parts of the body. Are we back into foreplay?

Furthermore, there are all manner of outlines. Some slap down their idea on a sheet of paper and are good to go. Others start out with something small and then keep reworking and extending it until by the time they are finished they have a first draft.

So who is right?

They all are.

We really have to try them on to see what fits. If the short outline doesn't get us into the story, try working out a long one, and if a long outline starts to destroy our interest, try the slap-something-on-paper-and-go approach. And if even that is too much, skip it all and strike out for parts unknown. It all works. The main thing is, folks, if one way isn't getting it, try another.

This sounds so simple and obvious, and yet there are writers who believe this is a waste of their valuable writing time. I can't understand people who doggedly tread the same old path, getting nowhere, rather than try another way. Well, yes I can, because that's exactly what I did for so many years, and why it took so long to get published.

There are experienced authors who consider experimentation a waste of effort. We already mentioned how big name writers can get away with slop. When we are first accepted for publication, editors go over our work with a microscope to give it the best shot of bringing a return on their investment. But the more sales we have, the less our work is looked at. The result is many books that are bloated and poorly plotted by big name authors who are making big bucks and see no need to alter their writing habits.

But this is painting by numbers.

The artist plays with light and shadow to create mood, and uses colors and proportions to give depth. We develop our craft by trial and error. And if we want to be good, it's a continuing process. If one way is not working, folks, try another. In fact, try them all.

For the beginner I recommend at least a sketchy outline, something to pull out when you loose the signposts.

Just remember an outline is not a Moses tablet.

Rigidly follow it like it's cast in stone and you will ignore logic for storyline and lose credibility. Treat it as a road map. If you come to a new fork, go with it a bit, see how it works out. As we write with the forefront of our minds, our subconscious keeps churning away like a computer chewing over mathematical data. At unsuspecting times it slips us new solutions. We have to be ready to grab them because they often result in a better novel.

Storyboards

A more extensive use of outlines are storyboards. It's a way to visualize the relationship of individual scenes to the whole novel. The board part of it can be anything, a corkboard, a piece of Styrofoam, or even unused wall space that won't be disturbed while it is being used. Start off labeling a card or a Post-it note for the first scene, then list the events that take place in that scene. Keep it brief. One or two words that will trigger the idea. Place the scene on the storyboard and do the same with the second, third, and on to the last scene.

Opening scene

Jim Dandy arrives at Elderhostel
Description of town of Bolder Harbor
Description of hotel & checking in
Meets some Elderhostelers & roommate

Scene 2

Jim checks into the Elderhostel
Two women also checking in
Helps them with their bags
Old woman introduces herself and niece
Alice Atwater and Dodee Swisher
Jim goes to his room & description

Don't worry about the order or omitting something at this stage. It can all be changed as the story's written. When all the cards are in place, study them, shift them around—not only the cards, but the action taking place on each of the cards. Use different color pens to show the importance of events in the scene if that helps; or even use different colored cards. Eliminate or combine redundant scenes and those that add nothing to the story.

When we're happy with what's on the cards and their placement on our storyboard, install rear-end in seat and hands on keyboard.

Brainstorming

A new story idea that's just forming is a fragile spider web of disconnected thoughts. Ridicule can pull it apart. But if it's crystallized in our mind, and we have confidence in ourselves, brainstorming can help us focus in on the building blocks of a plot. We need one or more people we trust, preferably other writers, those who will throw out suggestions as well as point out pitfalls. We lay out the idea and bat it around. Everything is on the table, no matter how ridiculous; throw it up in the air and see what winnows out.

I used this technique when I was under a tight deadline for the third Elderhostel Mystery, *Tip A Canoe.* I had two weeks to come up with a synopsis and a month and a half to come up with a first draft. I brought a general outline to my writing critique group. In a half an hour of batting around, I could see my original idea would never work, but through throwing out new ideas we were able to came up with the essence of the plot I finally used. Without that brainstorming session I could easily have wallowed around in the mud for a couple of weeks and missed my deadline.

There is one other tool I used to meet that deadline.

Free Association

This is the most valuable tool I use.

I got the idea from Elizabeth Neeld's book, *Yes! You Can Write*, but it's also a management tool, used individually or in groups, where it's called hot pen or fast pen

It's a form of free association, a sort of self-brainstorming. I use it for everything, outlines, new chapters, plots, building characters, whenever I get stuck, everything.

We need a timer. And we need an idea, say, how to kill someone in an unusual way. We set the timer for five minutes, then write like hell. Whatever pops into our minds. Even if it's only, "This ain't working, Clyde." Do not stop for corrections or misspellings or to pet the cat. When the timer goes off, we write a sentence summarizing the main idea we got from the session. We reset the timer and do it all again. Finally do it a third time.

At one point in writing *Tip A Canoe*, trying to churn out three first draft chapters every two days, I did a free association almost at the start of every chapter, when I didn't know where I was going and often when I thought I did. I always got something out of it, even if it was only to clarify the direction I had decided to take.

I should tell you, folks, this is an acquired taste. The first few times I drank coffee it wasn't anywhere near as good as it smelled, but later on I got to like it.

So it is with Free Association. The first few times I didn't get much out of it except the thought I was wasting fifteen minutes of valuable writing time. But I kept at it and soon all sorts of plot twists and turns and ideas popped out, most not fully blooming until the third five minute set.

Now I use it all the time.

Almost everyone I get to try it for a week, comes back saying it opened up a new set of options for them. So I urge you to try it, and let me hear how you make out. We all need feedback.

Beware of Naysayers

Like ridicule can pull apart a half-formed spider-web idea, so it can destroy the start of a writing career.

Most people can't conceive of knowing someone who makes money writing fiction. Consequently, the reaction we'll often get when we announce what we're trying to do is one of raised eyebrows. People will talk about it as our thing, our hobby, what we are into as if we're building model railroads. Those who read our early work will either become instant critics who tear everything apart, or gushing friends who love it all. Neither is helpful. The answer is, except for spouses and other writers, don't tell them. After talking about brainstorming this might seem paradoxical, but who knows if and when we'll finish our novel, much less get published? Fiction writing is damn hard work. We don't need to add their discouragement on top of it.

Beware of Me as a Naysayer

Also treat this book as a possible naysayer.

What I'm trying to do is point out the things that will give us the best shot at getting published. But this is a crazy business. There are no formulas.

And—surprise—I am not God.

Anything done well and with finesse can break any rule and still work. So if what I say here is contrary to what you believe is right for you, go with your gut.

However, if your way is not working, give some of these things a try. It's better than plowing the same old row.

About first drafts—somewhere in the middle the garbage starts to come alive, and I can hear my voice, and suddenly I start to believe it can work.

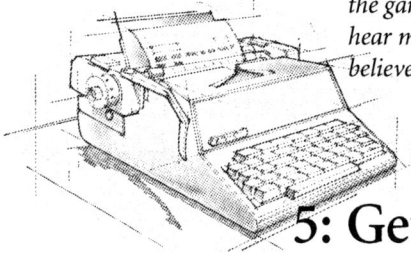

5: Getting It Down

First Drafts

Most beginners plan on writing one fantastic draft and then waiting for an agent to auction it off for big bucks. I know I did. But very, very, very few people write publishable first drafts.

Notice the word, "very?"

It is a useless word that conveys nothing.

On the second draft I would say: If you compare the population of No Trees, Texas, to New York City, you'd have the ratio of publishable first drafts to those that are not. I'm in the "not" class.

So what are we trying to do with the first draft?

Just—get—it—down.

Some authors, like Lawrence Block, rewrite as they go along. If that works, fine. But not for me. Nor do I recommend it for those of us who are beginners. We could end up rewriting forever and never reach the end. And until we type that last line, we don't have a novel.

The absolute minimum word count for a novel is forty thousand. I keep track of word count when I'm writing a first draft and forty thousand is always a magic number for me. Once I pass that and still have chapters to go, I know I'm okay. It's not hard and fast, but the conventional word count range for a novel is from sixty thousand—for thrillers and mysteries—to one hundred and ten thousand—for some science fiction novels. I recommend a word count for a first novel in the seventy to ninety thousand range. If it's too long the cost to the publisher goes up; it's just one more factor in figuring out the bottom line.

So, folks, for a first draft, just get it down.

I hate them myself. With first drafts every line and paragraph is a new decision, and every page is stepping into the unknown. I am always tempted to quit partway through. Sometimes only dogged persistence keeps me going when I want to scream—*this is all vulture dung.*

Then I remind myself that first drafts are closer to junkyard than showroom, and their sin is their saving grace. Since we know we'll need a rewrite, we can forget about trying for perfection and relax, kick off our shoes, air out our toes, and let our imaginations run free.

Think of a first draft as a complete outline.

But if we started with an outline, now is the time to put it aside. If we allow ourselves to be ruled by a Hitler-like outline, we'll go goose-stepping along rigidly focusing on a narrow path to a contrived ending. An outline will never prepare us for all the problems that will arise as we pace through our story and come to know our characters more deeply. Ignore those problems and we distort real world logic for the sake of the storyline, dooming our novel to the same fate as the thousand-year Third Reich.

A more American way is to go with the flow, hang loose, see where the road takes us. If we're successful in bringing our characters alive, we're never sure how they will react to one another, and the logic of this often sends us in a new direction. Remember also our subconscious will keep mulling over the story problems and will slip us new solutions if we're ready to accept them.

When I was writing *Killing Thyme* and found things getting boring, I solved it by doing someone else in.

Bump somebody off?

Hey, it's not as good as sex, but it does get the blood flowing.

Keeping Notes

One of the dynamics of changing things as we go along is we have to keep notes. If halfway through we need our hero to make a fast getaway, we better go back to an early chapter and mention he owns a Ferrari. If we need to change a woman from Nordic blonde to a chocolate-skinned West Indian, we better make sure we change it everywhere. We can't say that her makeup washed off to reveal... What if our story works better if we kill someone using a bazooka rather than a knife?

> Sam pulled out his knife, which was really a bazooka, and blasted a hole in the Ford Ranger, which was really a battleship?

Oh, yeah, that works.

We can change these things immediately, or make a note to correct them before the next draft. Since I am always on a hell-ride to complete the first draft, I make a note and keep on charging. Who knows, I might change back to the original before I'm finished. But we better keep notes, folks, or we'll forget, and inconsistencies will turn our readers off faster then a three-day-dead fish being eaten by a skunk on a hot summer day. No hyperbole here.

Keeping notes is simple if we do it as we go along. Some writers keep them on a pad beside the computer, or on storyboard cards if they are using them. I keep mine on a separate computer file where I can quickly add and retrieve such things as: character names and descriptions; things I need to go back and change; snippet ideas for future chapters; and stuff—names of restaurants, the protagonist's car. I also try to keep a timeline, what chapters take place on what days. This helps in case I need to refer to a past event—I hadn't seen Sally since she slipped me a Mickey on Saturday night—and it's major help if I have to alter a scene later on.

Suppose our subconscious tells us to bring back a character we set up as a one-show bit player. If we haven't seen this guy in five chapters, we may not remember his name. Or what he looks like. If we've been keeping notes we just pop out to our file. No problem. If not, we have to go though chapter by chapter and line by line until we find it.

Suppose our book is published and our editor wants a sequel? This is after we've started a completely new novel and haven't looked at our old one for over a year.

Remember our comment about inconsistencies? If Sally had two little girls in our first book, they better not turn into two teenage boys in the second.

If we've kept notes and character profiles, we can pop out to them and we're ready to go.

If not, we'll have to dig out the information by struggling line by line through our novel.

Guess which is faster?

Take notes.

Keep them around.

Stick with It

In writing a first draft, it's easy to give up. As I mentioned, I am tempted all the time. With every book.

Writing a first draft is a bit like running up a hill. The first time we're puffing and stumbling and sweating, with gravity enticing us to turn around. But if we hang in—and don't expire on the spot—we'll make it to the top. The next time we'll know we did it before and have a good chance of doing it again. The running may not get any easier, but each hill we climb gives us confidence for the next.

Once we have finally written the last line of our first draft, we can take joy in knowing we have the keel and ribs for our boat to set sail. Not the skin yet, and maybe not the driving force, but the first draft gives the final product it's form.

And we have done it.

We have written a novel.

We made it to the mountaintop, and the view is magnificent.

One of the big mistakes new writers make is trying to put the past all up front.

6: The First Leg of the Tripod

Plot

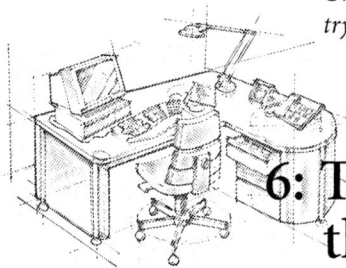

The basic plot of a novel is someone wants something and strives to attain it. One character: gets the hots for another, romance; is hired to steal secrets, action; sets out on a voyage, adventure; finds his life in jeopardy, suspense; or is confronted with a murder, mystery. They all contain a conflict that the character wants resolved. That goal is what propels the protagonist into action.

Story can be different from plot in that a story could be a flat-line recounting of the events. Plot is taking the story and pacing it in highs and lows to capture, hold, and increase the attention of our readers. It is the *what, how*, and *why* of who, what, where, when, why and how.

A mountain is the simplest way to describe a plot line. Let's place a character we can identify with, Oself, for our-other-self, at the mountain's base. The goal is to get to the top. The reason to achieve the goal could be anything, but Oself's need for it has to be paramount. Even life threatening. If Oself doesn't care, why should our readers care?

The most obvious thing is for Oself to hop in a Humvee, yank the sucker into four-wheel drive, and plow straight to the top.

Big whoop.

There is no conflict here.

No conflict, no story.

In Oself's quest for the top, he must continually face downturns of various intensities, mentally or physically, and overcome them, growing stronger each time until he's ready for the big climax. Each time Oself suffers a setback and overcomes it, our readers buy deeper into Oself's character. Oself has shown spunk and tenacity, he is an underdog who overcomes adversity, all traits readers can identify with. Soon Oself's quest becomes our readers' quest and they sign on for the journey.

So what we must do is to put something in Oself's way.

Can you say, "antagonist"?

This is the snarling beast from hell who is against us just because we are really good guys, swell looking, stouthearted, brilliant, brave, and humble. Oh yeah. The beast could be a man, woman, fate, the weather, or the mountain itself. The beast could even be the demons lurking in Oself's own mind. In plot, unlike football, it's not whether Oself wins or loses, but how well he plays the game. The outcome must be in doubt up to the very end. This keeps our reader pulling for our hero to succeed.

> I know your stomach's ripped open and your intestines hang out, both legs broken and an arm as well, one eye's swelled shut and your ear drums shattered, yet in spite of it all, Mr. Lucky, I know you can make it.

Which brings up the next point.

If we create an excess of obstacles the device becomes obvious.

We've all seen television shows where everything that possibly can go wrong, does, even to the point of nonsense. Our reaction? Just get the dumb thing over with.

Ever see a television hero rush from one place to another without encountering a traffic jam? You've heard of gratuitous sex? Meet gratuitous obstacles.

Major rule of thumb: Anytime a device becomes obvious, it is intrusive. And anything intrusive yanks our readers out of the action and destroys their pleasure of living in story-present. It is as effective as a long, dull sermon. We may not be able to sneak out of church, but our readers have no trouble in putting down our books.

Every little thing must not break against Oself or it will seem contrived. I had a critique of one of my books where the hero's sister is driving him home and he suddenly decides to go downtown. She's a pretty woman in the wrong lane and a man lets her cut in. What man wouldn't? The critique was that it was too easy and she should have driven around the block, but this has nothing to do with the real suspense of the story. To continually have every minor point go against the hero defies the odds of logic. Which is the next point.

The difficulties must be logical. Everything must play as real life or we'll lose credibility.

In *Total Control* by David Baldacci, one of the main characters retrieves a key to the door of her brother's house from a backyard fountain. Reasonable? Sure. Lots of people hide a single key in case they accidentally lock themselves out. But then we find the key ring also contains the key to the gun cabinet. Where's the logic here? To make sure if someone breaks in they'll have a gun to do the job right? If it contains the gun cabinet key, why not the one to the Mercedes as well? And the safe deposit box?

If we've done our job well and brought our readers into a state of suspense near the climax, we don't want to risk it all with something that is illogical, or something as clichéd as a traffic jam.

Okay, we are now ready to tackle the mountain.

Plot-line Mountain

The reason for climbing the mountain could be preconceived: his love is at the top; it's the entrance to the vault of the Holy Grail; just because it's there. But for our example, to show another way of doing it, let's let the opening situation dictate the need.

> Oself is out for a Sunday drive. He crosses a bridge on the wilderness road around Plot-line Mountain, but jams on the brakes when it's blocked by logs. Then the bridge blows up behind him. Then bullets zing off the Humvee's downhill fenders.
>
> In Cliché City we'd call this a situation.
>
> Suddenly Oself has a desperate need, not only for a restroom, but to get the heck out by the only way left open to him, over the mountain.
>
> Oself slams the Humvee into gear, yanks the wheel and mashes the pedal, spraying gravel as he bounds over rocks and humps and bumps, hell-bent on a yo-yo ride for the summit. Two hundred yards up he finds an old logging road out of rifle range and eases along. Birds sing

in filigree sunlight and all is right with the world.

Oh, yawn.

Then Oself barrels over a sudden crest that hides a deep wash and the Humvee soars like a cast-iron eagle. It mashes nose-down into the gulch. And Oself, neglecting to wear a seatbelt, no doubt earning him a traffic citation, crashes against the windshield. The birds now sing inside his head.

Then the Humvee starts rolling downhill, backwards, toward a sheer drop-off. The brakes no longer work. And the door won't open. On either side. Oself hops in the back and by punching and kicking and cursing and—when all else fails—praying, breaks open the tailgate. He dives out pancake-flat into a bed of thorns. The Humvee scrunches over him, wheels straddling his body, and plunges off the cliff. The silence of the idyllic day returns, for a few moments, until there is a crunch of metal meeting stone. Followed by an explosion. A black cloud rides an updraft to waft away in a gentle breeze.

Sssssonofagun.

Our hero climbs up the gulch to where the logging road continues on the other side. The grade is easy once more. A lazy zephyr dries the sweat on his brow. A chipmunk complains at his passage.

> Our readers' eyes start to glaze.
>
> Oself ventures onto an outcropping to check out the view when tiny puffs blossom at his feet, sprouting sprays of rock shards. Say what? A rifle crack echoes in the mountain air. And again.
>
> Holy excrement—or whatever—someone is shooting at him.
>
> Oself dives for cover and lands in a rocky gulch, bashing his knee. Oh darn. And breaking his elbow. Oh pshaw. And loose stones send him sliding down an escalator to hell. Egad gazooks.

Weeeell, you get the picture.

The overall theme is for Oself to make it to the summit. The times of excitement are interspersed with an easier road to give the reader a breather. But everything we do should point to the summit. Then as we reach it, just before the climax, we really ease off to where everything appears to be going Oself's way. This is a set up, of course, and not an absolute, but it can make the finale more satisfying. If a thunderstorm slips in on a cloudy day, who notices? But have the sun suddenly blackened by an anvil cloud and we've made an impression.

> Oself breaks out of the briers and brambles and only a fifty-foot grassy slope separates him from the summit. The air is clear. The birds are singing. Everyone can relax.
>
> Then out jumps a ten-thousand-pound grizzly. With a rifle. A great altercation takes place. There is weeping and

gnashing of teeth—talk about Cliché City—as well as kicking and clawing, until finally, ta da, our stouthearted Oself logically—always logically—defeats the bear. Or, alternatively, Oself could lose, but gain great insight, such as what the inside of a bear looks like.

We're not like those phony Hollywood guys; we can take the tough endings.

The Finale

A word about the finale. It is the high point of the book. The whole reason our readers set out to follow the rainbow is to find this pot of gold. Every twist and turn along the trail should progressively build toward this one magnified event, either preplanned as we work out an outline, or redesigned once we see where our first draft has taken us. In fact, some authors write their finale first and the rest of the book around that. I'm told Mickey Spillane worked like this.

Either way, our readers made this journey to the mountaintop with us, now we need to make sure they enjoy the view. We need to dramatize the scene as completely as we can without making it intrusive. Nothing should take place off screen and then be explained by a gathering afterwards. The action must answer the original question of why we set out on the journey—who is trying to kill Oself on Plot-line Mountain and why. We wrap up most of the secondary questions as well, but not necessarily everything. In real life we don't come away with all the answers, but we better make sure we answer the big ones.

I've read books where an author leaves the main theme hanging to entice the reader on to a sequel. Sort of like the non-fiction cliché, *more about that later*. I've never gone on to find *more about that later* because I was unsatisfied with the more that went on before. Each book has to be treated as an entity in itself.

Finally, the ending must be satisfying. Happy, sad, even inconclusive, our ending must leave our readers satisfied they made the journey with us. Cheat them on the finale and we'll walk the next journey alone.

Fast Fade

Once the climax is over, get out.

> Oself rides off into the sunset.

Don't drag it out.

> Oself stopped at Aunt Martha's for a piece of blueberry pie, washed his horse, polished his boots, and rode off into the sunset, meeting a blond with a figure like a brick excrement house, whereupon he altered his destination for Cliché City.

Plot Points

Plot-line Mountain is, of course, a metaphor for all plots. The first significant event is the roadblock followed by the bridge blowing up and bullets zinging off the Humvee's fender.

This is our first plot point.

The story's direction is changed from a Sunday drive to an immediate need to get away from the shooter, and an eventual need to escape over the mountain. When the first plot point is overcome, things smooth down, then Oself plunges his Humvee in a ditch. Again the story's course has changed, and intensified. He is on foot with something chasing after. The overall challenge remains until the end, but there are many events to change and intensify the climb.

All the ups and downs test Oself's character. Each downturn requires Oself to make a decision. In our simplified case, to turn back or forge ahead. And with each tough ascent Oself buys deeper into the project. The philosophy of coming-too-far-to-quit blossoms from desire into determination and then to obsession. This in turn increases our reader's resolution to hang in with him until the journey's end.

It's like watching hopeless Underdog in a football game. With the first setback we might shrug, but then Underdog makes a score. Holy cow, maybe Underdog has a chance. Another setback and Underdog fights back. Keep this up and by the end of the game we're pushing the television across the room in an attempt to get Underdog to the goal line. But let either team rack up a stack of unanswered touchdowns and we're flipping channels to catch Julia Child cooking squash.

Blocking the Story

Each adversity should generally increase in intensity, but not so relentless that it becomes obvious. To block out how the plot points might work, let's take a made-up story and look at those events that change and alter the course of the world, to use the ending of the old Paramount newsreel, the *Eyes and Ears of the World.*

- On an easy Sunday morning the island nation of Og is bombed. Plot Point 1.
- Ships and planes are smashed and sinking, blocking Og's operational forces. Through hard work, the debris is cleared away. Small victory.
- Enemy ships suddenly appear and a beach is invaded. Plot Point 2.
- Through a major effort the Oggies drive back the invaders. Hoorah, apparent total victory.
- But the invaders establish a beachhead across the island. Plot Point 3.
- Major problems now. Oggies rush troops into the fray and beat back a breakthrough, confining the enemy to a small beachhead. Minor victory.
- Enemy troops pour in and capture a town, committing atrocities. Plot Point 4.
- Oggies make a raid into the town and rescue the refugees before falling back to a fortified position. Tiny victory.
- Invader's planes bomb Oggies positions and enemy troops spread their perimeter. Plot Point 5.
- Oggies set up feint and make a counter charge, capturing a chunk of enemy troops. Bigger victory.
- Enemy bombs again and tanks throw Oggies way back. Plot Point 6.
- Captured invader troops reveal enemy will land planes at a captured airfield. Oggies recapture the field and surround it to capture the landing planes. Small victory with major potential.
- Invader personnel discover Oggies and try to warn invader planes. Plot Point 7.
- Enemy planes do not get message and land. Big battle and Oggies capture planes. Major victory.

- Invaders make mad dash to recapture planes and airfield. Plot Point 8.
- Oggies use invader planes to bomb the crap out of them and push them back to beachhead. Everything smelling of roses.
- Reserve invader troops and ships come pouring into beach creating a breakout. Plot Point 9.
- Oggies, in a desperate attempt, send planes to bomb invader fleet, sink some, cripple the rest and send them scurrying from the scene. Major desperate victory.
- Without backup, communications, and support, enemy troops fall into total disarray and surrender. Plot Point 10.
- Complete victory and story's conclusion.

Notice that each plot point defines a juncture where the story shifts and intensifies, requiring decisions by the defenders. Battle seesaws, but the victories and attacks are not boringly equal. You could make a case that each reaction to a plot point is a plot point in itself, and I would not argue, but these are the major ones. We could create a whole bunch of minor plot points by telling this through a lot of individual characters: a general in a shower as the first bombs fall; a construction worker dodging bullets to clear away the debris; a nurse treating the wounded in an enemy breakout.

But isn't this like using a storyboard? We can tack up a card for each plot point and move them around, not only in relation to one another but also in relation to the characters telling the story.

Author Dave Poyer once showed me how he blocks out a complicated storyline on a large poster, with lines and arrows connecting many secondary plots and many viewpoints where characters intersect, until they all came together at the conclusion.

How we do it, and *if* we do it, is our choice.

So, how many plot points or downturns should there be?

I'm tempted to cop out here and say: how ever many it takes to tell the story. I think a novel with less than six has a thin plot. But suppose it does? I would look all over to see if I made it too simple, and if I could integrate some new twists and turns. What I would *not* do is throw something in willy-nilly just to get another downturn.

Most big sellers have seven to ten plot points. The movie *Presumed Innocent*, for example, has twelve major plot points and a bunch of minor ones.

In *Tip A Canoe* I have at least eleven major plot points but, folks, I did not start out counting them. I wrote the story as it came to me and did a quick count just for this book.

Tip A Canoe, by the way, is a cozy mystery and some of the plot points are subtle compared to the battle of Og, but the principle holds whether it's a battle, a man fighting for his farm, a woman romancing a lover, a father searching for his son, or the police chasing a killer. Just plug in the events in place of the above.

One major danger here.

I've alluded to this above and I've said this before.

All the events must be logical and the result of character action. No angels saving the day, no miraculous rainstorm putting out fires, no adding cliché traffic jams for spice. This is a house of cards we will build in our readers' minds. A false wind will blow it down. And anytime a device becomes obvious it becomes as intrusive as an unflushed toilet. It yanks our reader out of story action, destroying his pleasure of living in the dream.

So that's the skinny on plot.

For those who think characters take over, remember whose hand is on the keyboard.
—Lawrence Block, at the Washington Independent Writers Spring Conference

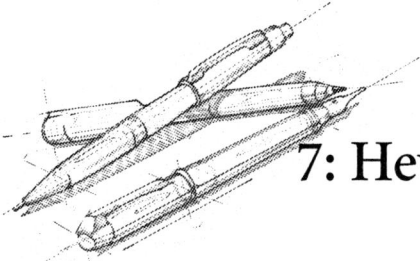

7: Hey, Who Are You?

Characterization

In some ways characterization should probably be placed before plot. A lot of writers work on characterization before they do anything. They find out who their characters are, put them in a place of confrontation, and see how they react. Nothing wrong with that. It allows us to add character bits and pieces as we go along.

I work on characterization after I finish my first draft. I used to think I was alone in this, but after making an unscientific poll, I've concluded it's about half-and-half. The British writer, John Braine, *Room at the Top*, advocated this approach. Barbara D'Amato, in one of her lectures at a "Dark And Stormy" conference, said she doesn't begin to know her characters until she's walked with them awhile.

Either way, sooner or later, like death and taxes, we have to work out the development of our characters. It is the *who* of who, what, where, when, why, and how. There is a reason for the *who* being placed first. Without *who* we have no story. Unless we develop lifelike characters with hopes and fears, strengths and weaknesses, how can we elicit a reader identification response? Draw cardboard characters and who will care what happens to them?

What's our reaction if we hear an old-time movie star has died?

Probably a big ho-hum.

But suppose that star had stopped and talked to us? Suppose we met her again, told her some of our life experiences and heard some of hers? That she was orphaned at four, shuffled from house to house, waited tables to earn money for acting lessons, and that men treated her badly before her big break. We identify with her ups and downs, admire her tenacity, and swap jokes and laughter along with our stories. Now we know her. Now she is a friend. Then we find she has been murdered.

What is our reaction now? Shock. Disbelief. Rage. Loss. And maybe we'll cry.

That's the reaction we want from our readers, folks. That's the difference between cardboard characters and those with substance. Between ho-hum and an Oself, our other self, response. And that's what will plug readers into our writing, and what will keep them coming back like a longtime friend.

To build characters like this takes almost as much work as writing another story, and most people regard it as a waste of time when they could be at real-writing. Characterization is real-writing, folks. It is not an adjunct. Not an option. You must get it right or you will continue to waste your effort on plot and rewriting.

I remember a professor pointing out in a critique of one of my unpublished novels that only one character was well rounded. It was the antagonist. The bad guy. I've since learned that we do a better job on the antagonist because we dislike the guy so much. But the protagonists (Oself) are only sketchily drawn because they are *us*, our other selves. We can see ourselves clearly, like in a mirror, and know ourselves intimately. What we fail to do, folks, because of our familiarity, is to get it down on paper so the reader can see—no, experience—Oself. We want our characters to grow on us during the story, so that we know more about them at the end—what they do and why they do it—than at the beginning. My professor failed to tell me how to do that. And I guess I was too dumb to ask.

So how do we do that?

If we want to reveal our characters to our readers, we must first reveal them to ourselves. To do that we give them a history, who they were before the story started.

Character History

Everybody has a history, a mother, father, a place they grew up. A character has to have a reason for living that is completely different from the plot.

What is his place in the world? What does she do for a living? Real people don't stumble around without a means of support. Their occupations color the way they think and act, whether they engage in these occupations during the story or not. Where does she come from? This is reflected in the way she speaks. What are his hobbies and interests? What are her dialogue tags, those often-used phrases and comments? What are the little mannerisms and quirks that he picked up in life? What are his goals and why are they important to him? Remember Oself's desire to reach the mountaintop? What inner conflicts, strengths and weaknesses, are aids and obstacles in attaining the goal? Even the strongest of us have doubts and weaknesses; even the weakest of us have strengths. What does his home look like? How does she make love? Or not make love? All these things make up the ghosts that hide in the corners and crannies and closets of our minds, just waiting for the right stimulus to pop out and yell: *surprise.* So must they be for our characters as well. It's what makes us tick.

We won't use all of the history in our main story, but all the material we gather will help us see our characters more clearly. The more clearly we see them, the more clearly they'll come across on the page, and as we move through succeeding drafts we'll find spots where bits and pieces of background, quirks, body language, odd sayings will naturally fall into place. One of the reasons I do characterization after the first draft is the same reason I hold off on my research, to forestall the temptation to add things just because I worked so hard to get them.

I think this may be a good time to state an axiom that I'll repeat throughout the rest of the book:

> Our writing should contain only that which advances the plot, adds to the characterization, or gives us a sense of place.

Print that out and tape it to the top of your monitor.

Just as we don't use all the history in our main story, so, obviously, we don't do a full history treatment on every character in the story. That's reserved for Point-of-View (POV) characters, those people whose heads we inhabit. Anything less than the full Monty here will seriously weaken our story. And not far behind are the main characters that are integral to the story's outcome. From here we move down in degrees to important minor characters, minor characters, and walk-ons, those who have no dialogue and only appear as background, little more than a subliminal blip on the mind.

But even with walk-ons we can dab a splash of color.

> The doorman got them a cab.

Black and white, right? Just facts. Suppose we embellish it with a few words.

> The doorman summoned a cab with a
> brass police whistle.

That tad of specificity not only gives us sound, the warbling of the police whistle, but that it's a brass whistle tells us the place is either up-scale or the doorman pretentious. Attention to small details can add much to a story. Its sense of place, or verisimilitude, the feeling of actually being there. Is it worth spending the extra four words? Your call. But if we have to bring the character back for another appearance, a whistle, a quirk, a mannerism will tag the character in for our readers.

So the history reveals characters, but we still have to define them.

Building the Character

There's more than one way to build a character.

Some writers incorporate everything about each person as they introduce them in their first draft. Of course this is far more than the reader needs or even cares to know, especially as it completely stops the action as each character comes onto the scene.

Imagine a play or a movie where a man is slapping a woman around and a policeman charges in to rescue her. He runs halfway across the stage, stops, and proceeds to tell everyone all about himself as the poor woman gets slapped around.

But for these writers it works. It gives a complete picture of each character as they go through their first draft but, folks, then they go back and cut out all the leftovers for the second draft.

Other writers I know, some with many published books, do it by continually reworking the story, adding bits and pieces of their characters' past lives as they go, until they bring them to life on paper. Obviously this works for them, but it doesn't quite work for me, and I suspect it will not work for someone starting out who is already trying to juggle a zillion balls in the air.

Still others base their characters on people they know, either from real life or from the movies and this keeps them focused as they build their stories. The only danger here is duplicating the character to the point of being libel. Not likely.

Finally, I know a writer who builds characters and plot organically from an event. This is similar to the authors described in chapter three who keep meticulous notes on various ideas, adding to them, until one idea reaches critical mass and the writers go to work. These writers work from a list; the single-event, organic approach is more pictorial.

We draw a circle in the center of a large sheet of paper for an event that's captured our interest, say the hot air balloon festival in New Mexico. From this we draw a line for our main character. Who is she/he?

Say, a woman balloonist. As we think about her over the course of the next few days, weeks, months, we put down what comes to mind. Give her a nickname, Sky. Say we make her a balloon gypsy, living out of an old van, working on the cheap to take tourists for balloon rides when she can swing it, odd jobs when she can't. She's now in her thirties, but Sky ran away from an abusive home to follow balloons when she was a kid. So from Sky's line we branch off to another for her mother. Call her Sarah. She ignored her husband's abuse until one day she whacked the guy and served five years for it. She's a little nutty now, hates men, and works as a waitress in New Mexico where the festival is, so she comes into play. We have to branch another line off from Sky's for her father and what he was like, and branches off from either of them for others who played in their lives, lovers, friends, siblings.

We go back to our balloon festival event and draw a new line for another major character. Say the balloon owner Sky flies for. Call him George. He owns four balloons and a string of fast food joints that he advertises on the balloons. Say he's married—so we'll need a line for his wife—but always hitting on Sky—so maybe we'll have another line for his impressions of Sky—and hits on whomever else might be walking by.

And perhaps George has a fat lecherous friend, Luther, who wants to ride in the festival and George assigns him to Sky's balloon. We can either make him branch off of George's line, or a line of his own from the festival event, or from Sky's, depending on who he affects the most. Maybe connections to all three.

And so it goes.

We not only put down the backgrounds and connections to one another, but what they look like, if they pick their noses, whatever traits come to mind as we think about what they would do and how they would act, so we could end up with something looking like streams leading into rivers which dump into our balloon-circle lake. We keep building these characters and when they overwhelm us, we open our festival event, put them in play, and see what develops.

I haven't tried this yet, but obviously it works. They all work. So how do I do it?

I build character profiles.

It's when they become almost as complex as one's own personality that the fine excitement begins. Because then they are not really characters any longer—they're beings, which is a distinction I like to make. A character is someone you can grasp as a whole, you can have a clear idea of him, but a being is someone whose nature keeps shifting.

—Norman Mailer

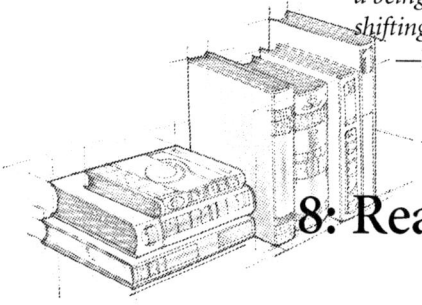

8: Real People

Character Profiles

I build character profiles using a list of background characteristics, some of which were given to me by my friend author Marcy Heidish, some of which I worked out for myself. How much I fill out depends on the importance of the character. This can be time consuming because, as I mentioned before, it's a bit like writing another story.

Name

What's in a name? A lot. It's the identity of our characters. Remember when making up the list of names to make sure that each character has a name that is easily distinguished from all other characters. Even so, we don't want to choose names without thought, especially for the main characters. Try to pick names that will fit the character. This will reinforce the character in the reader's mind. Want a strong character, give him a strong-sounding name. Judd. Short and jabbing. Mark is good, and if we want to soften it a tad, Marc. Aloysius on the other hand probably won't cut it, but it might be good for a balding jeweler with a paunch. Something plain? How about Jane? Ah, that's a too easy. But we can run across the grain as well, using Jane for an extraordinary woman. Hank is good, but it also carries with it a less sophisticated connotation. Again, we can cross-grain it.

What would we use for a rummy Englishman who runs a small publishing company, someone who is also a friend of man? How about Barley Blair? Barley gives the feeling of those things that go into the making of Scotch, and yet it has a friendly sound. John Le Carré chose it well for the main character in *Russia House*. I chose Jim Dandy because I wanted a name easy to remember and because in his first appearance he's grousing about everything and this gives him one more downer among strangers, a name everyone can use to make fun remarks, and grousing about it gives us a picture of what it might be like growing up with that name.

When you choose a name, say it aloud. How does it sound? Notice the names above, Barley Blair and Jim Dandy. A two-syllable name goes well with a single syllable, regardless of the order. Bart Hart sounds harsh. Jonathan Hart, however, was used very well for a wealthy, sophisticated, likeable character on the television show, *Hart to Hart*.

Where to find names. I collect them from obituaries; it gives me a chance to collect names both for their sound and nationality as well. There are lots of baby naming books, and there are also two others I keep around: *The Name Game* by Albert Mehrabian, National Press Inc., 7200 Wisconsin Avenue, Bethesda, MD 20814; and *Writer's Digest Character Naming Source Book* by Sherrilyn Kenyon.

Physical Description

The character's appearance is more than eyes, ears, nose, and throat. Everybody has those. It's the differences that we notice immediately. Cut off a person's nose and I guarantee you people will spot that right away. We can also use appearance to give us a foretaste of the character.

Here is a great description by Janet Evanovick from her novel, *Four to Score*:

> If people were cars, Lula would be a big, black '53 Packard with high gloss chrome grille, oversized headlights, and a growl like a junkyard dog. Lots of muscle. Never fit in a compact space.

This one from *Sins of the Brother* by Mike Stewart:

> (He) looked like he tried to kiss a moving train.

This one from *Bloody Bonsai*:

> Barny came in from the patio, unzipping a leather bomber jacket, holding himself erect, like he had spent too many hours on a military parade ground.

This parade-ground erectness allowed me to tag Barny so when he returned after a couple of chapters, I could immediately identify him for the reader by saying he came parading down the hall like he was counting cadence under his breath.

One other thing about physical description. If we are going to use it, we use it up front. Wait three or four pages and our readers will already build their own picture of the character and ignore ours. No big deal unless the description is integral to the plot.

What do we mean *if* we describe him?

I seldom describe my main character. I want to do all I can to have my readers identify with the main character. I know they will picture him from his actions so I try to stay out of their way.

You don't believe this? I'll give you six words and you draw a picture in your mind:

"My name is Bond, James Bond."

Confess, who do you see?

Sean Connery probably. But maybe Roger Moore or Pierce Brosnan. And yet Ian Fleming described James Bond as looking like Hoagy Carmichal, a thin, almost-emaciated old-time song writer and piano player; but no one ever pictures Bond that way. Incidentally, if you rent the old Bogey movie, *Key Largo*, Carmichal is the piano player in the picture.

For one more example, a writing teacher I had one time, Francis Fugate, handed out a story he had written and asked his students to read it. At the next class he asked them each to describe the main character. They all had vivid pictures, all different, but Fugate never described the character. And yet, when we mention characterization to most beginners, they think description.

Personal History

As we said, everybody has a history. Nobody drops out of the sky. Was he abused as a child? Did she become a prom queen? What side of the tracks did they live on and what did their parents do for a living? This history doesn't have to be in story form, just bare-fact statements, whatever works for you. It's the history that gives reason to the character's why-he-does-what-he-does. It can be as extensive as you like, but it must be at least enough for you to know the character's background.

Place in the World

What does she do for a living? Is she married, single, have children, where does she live? What is his health, financial status, and what clothes does he wear? In what social circle does she travel? All these things are interrelated and help to make up the outward appearance of our character. It may also reflect his upbringing, or contrast that upbringing, making him either a failure or a self-made man, depending on his background.

Goals

Everyone has hopes and desires. Even the proverbial couch potato dreams of an independent income so he can go on being the proverbial couch potato. For the protagonist and antagonist, the goal is what's driving the story. For lesser characters, their goals may round out their personalities, or add to a sub-plot.

Hobbies and Interests

You think these things don't matter? If we are trying to create a burly truck driver, a crass and foul-mouthed bumbler, chances are he will be more into bowling than ballet. But if he is into ballet it could be one of the things that round out him out. Why is he into ballet? A spinster teacher get him interested? Maybe seduced him as a boy? This type of thinking could spin into a story all its own.

Good grief, I'm telling you all my secrets and I'll lose some of my greatness. Ah, yes, but it might qualify me for the Humility of the Year award.

Quirks and Mannerisms

We all have these as well. Little ticks that we don't recognize because they are part of us. When I stand and talk to people, I usually find my hands folded in front of me. I knew of a man who kept punctuating his speech by blowing air out his nose, sort of an opposite sniff. I know another who's always rubbing his nose, and baseball players who are always adjusting their crotches. All of these things not only make up the characters and help us see them more clearly, but they can also be used as dialogue tags. If we have set up Oself so that he always rubs his nose, later we can say without fear of misinterpreting whose dialogue it is:

He rubbed his nose. "What a dreary day."

Strengths and Weaknesses

No one is all good or all evil. If you create a Superman you'll have a comic book character. That's not necessarily bad if that's the type of story you want. James Bond is such a character, and has done well, but it came out of a different era and has a sales record to sustain it. I think trying to break in with that character in today's market might be a hard sell. The same thing happens if you build the opposite, a shriveling weakling with no redeeming qualities. Hard to elicit dislike for a cardboard character, much less fear. But if he's also cunning, now we have someone who could be dangerous. Sometimes we try so hard to make a character hateful that we end up with one nobody believes in. I once built a nasty character, a pervert and a killer among other things, but he had two young daughters who he treated like gold. There's always a redeeming quality. We have to realize that even the most evil person doesn't think of himself as doing anything wrong. We need both traits.

Inner Conflicts

These are the things battling for possession of our characters' minds. We are privy to them in the minds of our Point-of-View, POV, characters, and see them in the actions of our non-POV characters. A lot of it ties back into *Personal History* and *Place in the World* topics. It's the conflict an elderly widower might face going on a trip where he will meet new people. He grouses about all the things that could go wrong, and yet he hopes it will turn out well. The conflict of a woman being set up for a date, hoping for someone special, but will fear of rejection make her turn it down for the safety of loneliness? Could a person's limited education keep him from mixing with people he'd really like to get to know?

Change

We've mentioned this before. What change takes place in the character over the course of the story? In his action, his makeup, his thinking. None of us can go through the near-death of a child, a major accident, a personal religious revelation, a love affair, a sea voyage, without it affecting us. Positive or negative. During or at the conclusion of our story, our characters should be changed by the experience even if it's only in a subtle way.

Dialogue Sayings and Comments

Like quirks and mannerisms, we all have things we say all the time, maybe without realizing it. Like: ya know; that's marvelous; what-a-ya-gonna-do; don't you know; and, Jim Dandy's favorite, great, really great. They can be one worders, phrases, or whole sentences. These things can be used not only to help define our character but, as dialogue tags, to identify them as well. My mother for a period in her life said, "With it." "I didn't spill the milk, Mom, it wasn't me." "With it." When someone asked why she said it all the time she couldn't believe she did. After that, we repeated it as a reminder every time she said it; it still took her six months to break the habit. But what a great tag. All we need is, "With it," and immediately the reader knows who is speaking.

Home

A house is a reflection of the people living there. If there are antimacassars on the furniture, and they call them antimacassars rather than doilies, doesn't that tell us something about who lives there? If photographs are plastered all over the door and on wallboards and stacked up on shelves, chances are a professional or serious amateur photographer inhabits the place. And if there's pots all over? Or paintings? If a woman keeps a casual or sloppy home we'll probably have a negative opinion about her right off, but if we find it's that way because of all the attention she gives to the children and her husband, our negative could be turned into a positive. Remember in *The Dead Poets Society* how the strict parent, whose son committed suicide, perfectly lined up his slippers under the bed? Didn't that tell us something about him, and why he refused to consider himself to blame for the incident? Whether a woman grows up in a mansion or in a dirt-floor shack will be reflected in her outlook for the rest of her life. Again, we might not do this for all our characters, but if we use the house as a setting, we need to carefully think about it as a reflection of our character.

Religion

What a person believes will color his outlook. A fundamentalist will probably not want to hear someone talking of Darwinism while a Moslem might not take an offered alcoholic drink. How much they believe or don't believe will affect a character's behavior and provide an internal conflict when he/she does something contrary to that code of ethics. Again, we might not actually bring it into play, but it will still make the character more real to us.

How Do They Make Love

Sex is so much a part of our makeup, how can we not take it into consideration? Does she do it in the afternoon, on rooftops, hanging from a chandelier? Is he obsessed with it, or just the opposite? Do they do it lovingly or clinically? Is it a pure power trip? Kinky, who's on top, grunt and groans, cries in the night. I remember reading about a boy who died suddenly in his gradeschool years and his mother lamented about all the things he would miss, one was that he would never make love on a rainy afternoon. Wow. Didn't that say something about the woman? And about the love for her son?

Humor

This one's hard to catalog. Very few people have no sense of humor, even if what they have is warped. If you are trying to build a likeable protagonist, an Oself character, better give him a sense of humor and, better yet, the ability to laugh at himself. A complete lack of humor will result in a cold-fish character.

Okay, that's it. Whew. It takes a fair amount of thinking and putting it all down. And we could go deeper into it if we wished, shoe sizes, how they like their coffee, what their grandparents were like, childhood friends, it all goes into the crucible. You can never know too much about the character. Again, most of this stuff doesn't get into the book, but will bring the character alive in your head and on the paper.

Do we have to do it?

Obviously not, because a lot of published writers don't.

But if you are starting out, or if you are not getting results another way, give this a try. I'm stressing it, folks, because after nine novels of flat characters, and half again as many years of writing, this worked for me.

Keep It Around

One more word of advice before we move off character profiles. After you work them up, save them. Keep them. Back them up on a floppy disk and put it in a cold dark place. You never know when a novel will turn into a series, and it will be of immense help to have the backgrounds of the main characters for the next book to build on. If your protagonist drinks black coffee in your first book and then takes cream and sugar in the second, someone will want to know why. As for the rest of the characters, you never know when you will need a similar character in the future, or use the background as a jumping off place, maybe combine it with another for a new character, or just as a reminder of how to do it. And remember that note file we talked about? Keep that around as well. Floppy disks are cheap. It is always easier to find something you saved in a note file than to dig it out of a novel. Save them. Save them all.

Marrying Character to Plot

Okay, once we've got our characters fixed in our minds, by any of the methods we discussed, it's time to integrate them into the story.

Want a good example of marrying character to plot? Read *The Music Room* by Dennis McFarland. I learned a great deal from it, about descriptions as well, and recommend it as a story and a study. In it he develops his characters, bringing in history and relationships as the story paces along.

That's what we want to do.

Let's take our old friend, Oself. Let's place him with three men outside an elevator, with people trapped inside the elevator. If the elevator doors open they will set off a bomb which is already ticking down from two hours. Help is three hours away. Everything depends on Oself and the three men because the high rise building is in the middle of a desert.

Hey, it's just an example.

So the first plot point is the discovery of the bomb. Oself and the men have the choice of defusing the bomb or slinking away like cowards.

Oself's for slinking.

Be a hero?

Fagetaboutit.

But the situation triggers an oft-remembered flashback of when he hid as a child in a closet while his mother was beaten.

The shame of that long ago incident keeps him from now being the first guy out the door. He'll hang. For an hour.

Then a young mother crying in the elevator pleads for her children.

This triggers another memory. Oself and his wife had a knockdown fight and he decided to leave her, but the children in the elevator remind him of his own children and his love for them. So he hangs some more.

And so it goes.

Oself's memories play off the reality of the bomb and the other three men. In the anxious moments as they sweat to defuse it, they share their stories with each other and with those inside the elevator, their hopes and fears and cowardly acts. Finally, all the sharing of stories builds a community bond so strong it overpowers any thoughts of individual self-preservation. Oself, not wanting to let these guys down now, grabs deep inside for an unknown courage and hangs some more. The last seconds ticking off lays bare his rawest emotions, the fear that has haunted him since hiding in the closet and caused him to run from everything, even now from those he loved, and he realizes the shame of that time has made him believe he is unworthy of anyone's love, which has kept him from bonding to his wife and children. This galvanizes his resolve. He is going up or down with these guys, those in and out of the elevator.

Then the bomb is defused.

Suddenly it's over. Oself is a hero, shouting and laughing and dancing with those who shared in the struggle, bound to them for the rest of his life.

And more than that, he has banished forever the ghost in the closet, and come out into the sunlight. He is free at last to love himself and those around him.

Okay, we have a lot of plot here, and of course we're *telling* everything rather than dramatizing it, but this is an example of how it's done. We don't stop the action and plop a character's whole background out on the table. That would be boring. We weave it in like colored thread as important points come up. Something triggers a memory and we get a glimpse of our character's past. This in turn helps us to understand why he does what he does. We see him in three dimensions.

We build characters the best we can, using the way that fits our personality. Then we weave our characters into our story. This is not a waste of time, folks, when we could be doing real-writing. Characterization is real-writing. It is not an adjunct. Not an option. You must get it right or all the time we now spend on rewriting will be a waste of effort.

All my life I've looked at words as though I were seeing them for the first time.

—Ernest Hemingway

9: Effective Writing

Spending Words

Writing is rewriting. That's a cliché, folks, but true. So we should think about setting up a principle:

> It should go without saying that if, after you have managed to conquer the principles of characterization, and spent a like amount of time working out an engaging, intricate plot, it will all be for naught if your writing is so laborious that no one will care to plow through it.

Do we agree with that?

Well, take a look at the principle. If it should go without saying, why do we need to say, "It should go without saying"? And why do we need to go through all the other flowery stuff that only belabors the laborious writing we're saying no one will want to plow through? So let's rewrite it as clearly and succinctly as we can.

> If you ain't got good writing, you ain't got nothing.

Well, okay, maybe it's not grammatically correct, but it does get the point across. And effective writing might not always be grammatically correct. It might contain fragmented sentences. It might use a descriptive word for a verb. But it should always contain only those words needed to get the idea across, and clear enough to be completely perceived.

We cut out forty words by the rewrite. Guess which reads faster? That's why the second sentence contains so much punch. If by rewriting you cut ten words a page, over 240 pages, say the length of *Bloody Bonsai*, you will have saved 2,400 words. That's a whole chapter. And if you lost nothing essential in the cutting, which reads faster? If you can save a word by rewriting a sentence, it's worth it. We could cut the above statement still more. "Bad writing equals nothing." But I don't think it's as clear and effective. Which gets us down to a real principle.

> Spend only those words necessary to make the story come alive.

This doesn't mean cutting out descriptions or backgrounds or dialogue or character interplay. What it means is squeezing out the fat to leave a rich, simmering broth. When they call a book a fast read, a no-put-downer, it's because the author has squeezed the maximum use out of every word. This requires cutting all redundancy, eliminating or combining sentences that have similar meanings, and replacing easy clichés with words that are fresh and carry an idea on more than one level.

> Dawn found them outside Baghdad! Their eyes were filled with the wonder of it (sand blown though they were), and it gave a "lift" to their spirits, which had been drastically, and almost permanently,

> seemingly totally depressed. They were still maybe one or maybe two miles away, "as the crow flies," but the fragrant smell of the city lovingly reached out to them, and the beauty of the city overwhelmed them till they were standing in "awe!"

Okay. Apparent things first. Parentheses are a lazy way of trying to make a sentence work when it really should be rewritten. They slow the flow, disturb the chain of thought, and I don't think they have a place in fiction. If they really fit into the sentence they can be replaced by commas or dashes. Then we have the words in quotation marks. If the word fits, the quotation marks are unnecessary, and if it doesn't, the marks will only call attention to it. Look at the exclamation points. An occasional use, like three or four in a novel might work, but an exclamation point won't give punch to a sentence that lacks it. And there are the clichés—*as the crow flies* and *awe*—which drain off any spontaneity we might have accidentally stirred up; they are the hallmark of hackneyed writing. What about all those adverbs and adjectives? They will not improve weak nouns or verbs, but they do weaken strong ones. Next are all the generalities that tell little and show nothing. Look at the words "seemingly" and "almost." In "almost" every sentence these appear you can leave them out without changing the meaning. Finally we have archaic usage and a clichéd sentence which started it all. "Dawn found them outside of Baghdad."

The cardinal sin of the paragraph is that it doesn't engage the reader. Let's see if we can straighten it out using our old friend, Oself, to give us focus:

> They galloped over a rise a half-mile outside Baghdad. A pink dawn silhouetted

> its domes and minarets, turning the desert city into a promise of rebirth. Oself rubbed grit from his eyes as a breeze brought him the sweet fragrance of jasmine, enriched by the tart smoke from camel-dung fires. A cock's crow announced the day, and Oself's doubts slipped away with the shadows of night.

Let's break this down and compare paragraphs. Instead of the passive ho-hummer, "dawn found them," we give it action that engages the reader. Something is going on. What is it? And we give color to the dawn, using it to paint a picture of Baghdad, further engaging the reader. Even the pink dawn is foretelling. We eliminate confusion by declaring it a desert city. Instead of adverbs and adjectives, we try for stronger verbs: silhouetted, brought, enriched, announced, slipped away. The promise of rebirth uplifts our spirits without the obvious telling us. In the third sentence we shift the emphasis from "They" to Oself, so that instead of telling our readers how to feel, we allow them to experience it through Oself's eyes. By replacing vagueness with the specific we not only give authority to our narration, but we trigger responses in our reader's mind. "Fragrant smell" from the first paragraph tells us nothing. But jasmine and smoke and dung evoke remembered aromas in our minds. Also, why spend words on whether we're two or three miles out? We are the God of the story. Half-mile. That's it. Who's going to dispute us? And finally, we let the reader experience Oself's mood shift and the reason for it at the end of the paragraph, setting us up for the beginning of the next.

What else makes this paragraph work?

Remember in chapter two we said our job is to coax out sensory memories that will trigger the imagination and life experiences of our readers?

This description engages the senses. Sight, sound, touch, smell. Only taste is missing and I tried to simulate that with the "tart draft," and contrasted it with the "sweet fragrance" to stimulate a known sweet and sour response in our minds. We often limit ourselves to visuals when we put things down on paper, but see how the use of the other senses multiplies the feeling of presence? We always want our readers to feel like they are right there, watching it happen, right before their very eyeballs. And nose, and ears, and tongue, and skin.

Cutting Out the Curlicues

We talked about spending only those words necessary to bring the story alive. There is a corollary principle that we've mentioned before:

> Cut out everything that doesn't advance the plot, add to characterization, or give a sense of place.

But suppose I wrote a story to show a religious principle, or make a political statement, or to point out a hidden truth, shouldn't I put that in regardless?

The obvious answer?

No, nein, nada, non, nyet, fagetaboutit.

Movies and books that set out to prove a point or make a statement and—forgive me—religiously hold to it, are almost always poor entertainment. A case in point is Michael Crichton's

Rising Sun. I read that book thinking how tight it was until somewhere in the middle the character suddenly starts talking about the Japanese economy taking over the world and for a number of pages it was like walking through chewing gum. It added nothing to the novel and was intrusive. The author departed from a good story to step in and state an opinion. It ruined a fast read for me, and history proved it in grave error.

Suppose we have an extraneous amusing incident or a funny bit of business that really is an aside to the story, do we leave it in or take it out?

If it contains a few words and is very funny, I'd probably leave it in. If it's a lot of words and only mildly funny, I'd opt to drop it. But only the author can make that call. And if we screw it up, it could cost us the chance to be published. That's why we make the big bucks. Oh yeah.

It's okay to start out with a premise, but once we get into the novel, if that premise no longer fits, it has to go. If we want to have a happy ending, but as we work it through everything points to a disaster, guess *wha-at*? Sure, we could force it, or phony it up, but it will be intrusive and jerk our reader out of the dream.

Each story rules how it will be told.

I often think of writing as an art, much like painting watercolors or sketching a beautiful landscape. It has to be unhurried to produce exquisite results. The wrong paintbrush or shade might destroy the entire work. How much poorer would all societies be had they not benefited at one time or another from the eye of the painter, sculptor, photographer or writer.

—Charlotte Austin

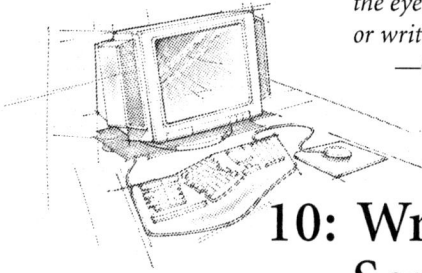

10: Writing Effective Sentences & Paragraphs

Active Sentences

Passive writing is to be avoided.

It's a tip-off the writer is a beginner. Passive writing, as in "passive writing is to be avoided," slows down our writing because it reverses the normal direction of speech.

> The wind blew John down. He crawled
> to the lee of a stone wall.

This is direct and has impact. The wind is the active agent. John is on the receiving end of the wind's action. The power part of any sentence is at the end, so the focus here is John getting knocked down. The normal progression would then lead us into John's reaction.

> John was blown down by the wind. He
> crawled to the lee of a stone wall.

Now things are reversed. By placing the active agent at the end, the impact is lost. The power position of the sentence now is the wind, leading us to believe we are talking about the wind rather than John.

Well, so what?

The *so what* is that the first sentence is a faster read because it not only contains fewer words, but because it follows in the natural flow of the way we talk. The second sentence slows us down because it requires us to collect the whole sentence before we can mentally assimilate what the writer's getting at. And because the wind is in the power position, the next sentence about John could jar us further, perhaps even causing us to stop and reread it.

What are we after again, folks?

Writing easy reading?

Then we have to do everything we can to keep our readers in the dream. Are they going to say, "Ho ho, look at the passive sentence"? Probably not, but it will not feel right and it will slow them down. And even if readers don't recognize passive writing, we can bet an agent or editor will.

Remember our clichéd sentence from our last chapter?

> Dawn found them outside Baghdad!

We can muddy it more by making it passive.

> They were found outside Baghdad by the
> dawn.

This is not only passive but it places the power on the dawn, which might be okay if we were going on to explain the morning, but what we're really after is the city and its effect on the travelers.

We can also introduce a passive sentence or clause using one of the *to be* verbs.

> It was like they were paddling in a world of their own.
>
> They paddled in a world of their own.

The second sentence, obviously, is the active one. Whenever we see *was/were* in our sentences, treat it with suspicion. They should be a red flag for us to look more closely. Are there times when we'll use them? Of course. We could write convoluted sentences just to avoid them, but that defeats the whole purpose.

Another thing about passive sentences, they often introduce weaker verbs.

> The winter sun was momentarily reflected off...
>
> The winter sun glinted off...

Glint saved us four words and gives us more impact. But it is the impact we're after more than the words.

> John was cutting his meat surgically.
>
> John's chubby hands pared the fat off his steak with all the skill of a surgeon dissecting a frog.

The first sentence uses an adverb to give us a vague indication of how John cut his meat, but the second sentence, while containing more words, uses specificity and illusion to show us what is happening.

Sentences with introductory infinite-verb phrases will also slow down our reading and sometimes stop it dead in the water, completely muddying our meaning.

> Pulling out his key, he turned the lock and opened the door.

This implies he turned the lock and opened the door while he was pulling out his key. A lot of beginning writers will use this sentence construction thinking it introduces a bit of art to their writing, but it is actually an archaic form used in the last century, and can be carried to ridiculousness.

> As he finished his chores, he rode downtown.

So, get rid of sentences with introductory infinite-verb phases, put the emphasis of a sentence at the end to lead into the following one, and rewrite the sentence at the beginning of this topic, "passive writing is to be avoided," into:

> Avoid passive writing.

Speed

We can control the speed at which our story flows by the length of our sentences. Want it to move fast, say for an action scene? Use short sentences. In the same way, should we want to stretch things out for a breather at the conclusion of some fast action, to vary the pace of the story, we can lengthen our sentences. It's nice to have a fast-paced story, but if it goes on relentlessly it will be tiring to read. Like everything else, vary the pace.

What we said for sentence length goes as well for paragraphs. Short paragraphs will give the feeling of reading faster, long ones will slow it down.

Dialogue will also read faster. It will slow the story in that the pace will slow down in order for the dialogue to take place, but it will read faster than narrative.

Paragraph Flow

We can provide flow from one paragraph into another by arranging sentences. The power part of the sentence comes at the end, as a lead-in to the sentence that follows it. The same thing holds true for a paragraph; we want to have our most important idea at the end to lead into the next paragraph.

> "We would have gone in with Clyde," Simon said, "except I knew he wanted to find out about the treasure they were taking off that old galleon. Phyllis wanted to do some shopping and sightseeing and we didn't want to be tied down."
>
> Harold jumped up from the table, knocking his chair over. "I got it," he said in a voice that boomed throughout the room.

The above sequence implies Harold flies out of the chair because something in that last sentence gave him a eureka moment, either the shopping and sightseeing, or being tied down. But suppose we actually wanted the business about the treasure to be the eureka moment? We rewrite the paragraph to make it the last thing before the outburst.

> "We would have gone in with Clyde," Simon said, "except Phyllis wanted to do some shopping and sight seeing. We didn't want to be tired down and I knew Clyde was into that old galleon and treasure thing."
>
> Harold jumped up from the table, knocking his chair over. "I got it," he said in a voice that boomed throughout the room.

We can do the same thing in how we order our words.

> He flipped on the living-room light to reveal a grand piano taking up the lion's portion of the room with two leather armchairs, a flowered sofa, and a walnut coffee table scrunched to one side.
>
> "Wow," Lacy said, crossing to the piano to run her hand over the keys. "This is a Steinway."

> He flipped on the living-room light to reveal two tanned armchairs, a flowered sofa, and a walnut coffee table, all scrunched to one side as a grand pi-

> ano took up the lion's portion of the room.
>
> "Wow," Lacy said, running her hand over the keys. "This is a Steinway."

By reordering the living room's items we provide a flow into the second paragraph and without the need to restate the piano. Take the following two examples:

> Jim collected olive oil in a foam cup, a large onion and, in a separate cup, a quarter of a teaspoon of saffron—short little yellow stems about the thickness of fine blond hair—and finally, in a third cup, three teaspoons of salt.
>
> "Be careful with that saffron," the chef said, "it costs eighty dollars an ounce."

> Jim gathered up a large onion and, in separate foam cups, olive oil, three teaspoons of salt, and the short yellow stems, resembling fine blond hair, of saffron.
>
> "Be careful with that," the chef said, "it costs eighty dollars an ounce."

We saved seventeen words by reordering how we collected the ingredients, and by working saffron into the last word of the sentence it flows into what the chef says in the next paragraph without actually reusing "saffron."

Take one more:

> Josh eased the small duffel to the floor and peeked into the living room: big stuffed chairs and a settee with a flowery pattern; a glass table with a telephone by the door to the dining room; framed oils on dappled green walls; a marbled fireplace with a portrait above; and a mauve carpet.

As it stands now our focus is on the carpet. Okay if the next paragraph starts off with Josh realizing that it's worth twenty-five thousand. But let's mentally rearrange everything so that the last entry reads:

> ...and a marbled fireplace with a portrait above.

Now we're interested in what the portrait's about.

> ...and framed oils on dappled green walls.

Now we're emphasizing either the framed oils or dappled green walls. While the walls are in the power position, our minds tell us there is not a lot of interest in walls so it's probably the framed oils. We could rearrange to leave no doubt:

> ...and, hanging on the dappled green walls, framed oils.

How about:

> ...and a glass table with a telephone by
> the door to the dining room.

This focuses our attention on the dining room, great if Josh is heading for it.

> ...and, on a glass table by the door to the
> dining room, a telephone.

Now it's more likely Josh is going to make a call.

So, as in sentences, placing the main idea at the end will naturally lead our readers into the next paragraph. Place it somewhere near the front and our reader will hesitate, a pothole in the road, because it's not what they are expecting.

How badly will it jar them?

Depends on how far removed from the next paragraph is it.

But we're not after acceptable here.

We're not talking about writing sort-of-easy reading.

We're talking easy reading.

Black Words on White Paper

We've said before we want to engage our readers. Show them the story picture. If we were artists we could draw a pen and ink sketch. As writers all we have is black print on white paper, but that doesn't mean we can ignore how it looks.

Imagine that we are in bed together...

Let me rephrase that.

Suppose our reader is in bed, late at night, bleary eyed, just finished a chapter of our book, and looks at the next page. It's solid print from margin to margin. That goes on for another page. And another page. And page after page.

Guess what the reader will do, folks?

And guess what will happen when they return the following night, tired, and look at that relentless block of print?

If we lose them that first night, we could lose them for all time.

Now contrast that with them turning the same page to a new chapter and finding a short paragraph. Maybe one sentence. Maybe only one word. Or a piece of dialogue. And we follow that by some more short paragraphs or dialogue, all of varied lengths. The eyes are drawn to the first line, just to see the connection with the previous chapter, and if we're good, that leads to the next line. Maybe they'll read the whole page, or just a paragraph. Either way, we have whetted their appetite so they'll be eager to return the following night.

Why should we worry about readers late at night?

Because if we can hold them at this time, think how we'll grab them when they're fresh. So let's give them some white space by varying the paragraph lengths. If a bit of business requires a lot of explanation, just break the paragraph in the middle. And if you don't think that works, throw in a bit of action or dialogue to interrupt it. "He blinked to clear his eyes and turned back to the bomb." Or even—"he blinked."

I think we should view our pages almost like a picture. This might be a crazy thing to say about writing, but our job is to marry our reader to the printed page. It's only black print on white paper. There's no color. No graphics. So we have to make it interesting in every way we can.

The same holds true for varying sentence length and structure. Here it's not so much of an overall visual effect as it is with paragraphs on a page. With sentences it's pace. If the cadence of one sentence is like that of the next, and the next, and the next, it goes on like the clickity clack of a railroad track, or the thump, thump, thump of expansion joints on an endless bridge. Read it aloud and check it out. If we repeat a cadence over a short section to deliberately pound something home, okay, otherwise the drone will bore our readers right to sleep.

Along with repetitive sentence cadence, we have a similar problem in word use. Using the same word two or more times on the same page is jarring. The mind stumbles on the redundancy and loses the flow, a bit like taking a sleepy ride on a rubber raft and jolting up against some unseen rocks.

But this is so elementary, who would do it?

Maybe not as we are writing our story, but how about when we come back for another draft? All we want to do is change one paragraph. Do we look at the preceding paragraphs and those following to see how it all flows together? Or do we just stick something in and go? This is the time words, and even phrases, get inadvertently repeated. So after we rewrite a sentence, we reread the paragraph, and then reread the whole page to see how everything flows.

This is a particular problem to those who work only on hard-copy. On a computer we can repeat the paragraph and work it to death, but on a hard copy the temptation is to effect a correction in the space between two double-spaced sentences. The other temptation is to squeeze in a fix that will not require the retyping of the next page, and maybe the rest of the chapter. If we can't do that, we might even decide the original page is good enough as it is.

It's not good enough, folks.

It's never just good enough.

Either it's the best we can make it or it's not. There is no back door to effective writing.

I don't like anything that takes me out of the dream and dumps me on the floor.
—Laura Lippman, reviewer and author at Malice Domestic 2000

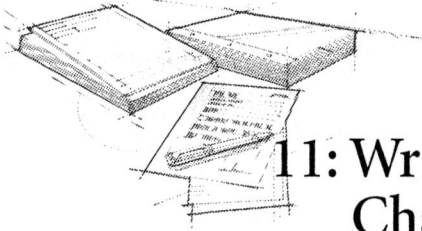

11: Writing Effective Chapters

From Chapter to Chapter

In the same way we have sentences flow from one to another, and paragraphs flow from one to another, we can have chapters flow from one to another.

> "So what do we do about the Marvel woman?" Miles asked.
>
> Josh swung to the thick-necked man sitting on the edge of his desk, small eyes squinting at him. "What do you want to do?"
>
> "I think we oughta call her. Try again, ya know." His lips spread in a yellow-toothed smile and his yellow eyebrows popped up like McDonald's arches. "So, want me to call her?"
>
> Josh held out his hand to reply, but a knock on the door interrupted him.

> They both turned to see Effie standing there.
>
> "She's here," Effie whispered. "Miss Marvel."

End of chapter, start of a new one.

> Effie stepped aside and Miss Marvel walked in.
>
> They were right.
>
> She was a "looker." Yeah, momma.

Chances are a reader in bed finishing one chapter and checking the next before she goes to sleep, will be enticed into this chapter because it is seamless.

This is the fastest and easiest read. That is not to say this is the only way. The closing of a chapter is a bit like the ending of a day. Tomorrow we start afresh. Only in real life we usually awaken in the same bed.

In fiction we can have the next chapter shift in time and place and into a completely different person's head. Television has predisposed us to this. How many of us grab the remote and channel-surf between commercial breaks? If we give our readers a couple strong clues as to where they are, they'll pick it up and travel on.

But, folks, the earlier in the book we change characters and/or time, the weaker this link is. If our reader in bed recognizes nothing in starting a new chapter, it's easy for her to put it down, so the hook into this new chapter better grab the reader where it hurts. Also, if we end the previous chapter with a cliffhanger, the reader will be anxious to pick up the thread again and will hang on for a chapter or two. If you have any doubts of what I'm talking about, watch where the commercial breaks are on television.

Either way, we need to place the power or climax of the chapter at the end so that when the narrative again picks up at this point, the reader will remember and be able to latch onto its continuation.

In the above example the chapter ends with Effie announcing Miss Marvel. Suppose we have two chapters now with different characters and location. When we come back, the way it's written, the reader should have no trouble picking it up. But if there's any doubt, if we are reintroducing characters that haven't been seen in awhile, we need to make sure our readers know who they are or we'll stop the easy reading flow. Nothing is worse than to have to flip back through pages of text to try to figure out who a character is.

How long should a chapter be?

As long or as short as we want. I think it's a good idea to have the first few chapters fairly short. If a reader picks our book off the rack and skims through a couple of chapters, they'll often feel they have invested time in it and will be more likely to buy. Shorter opening chapters facilitate that. Shorter chapters, like sentences and paragraphs, will also make the story feel like it's moving faster.

Finally, nothing of significance should take place between the chapters. If ten months elapse between chapters, obviously the world goes on, the protagonist gets older, things change, and that's okay so long at it's not a story event.

If one chapter ends with a detective giving up on a case and going to Europe for a year's vacation, and the next chapter starts with him returning, the time in Europe can be given in a quick summary. But we better not find out that, while he was gone, the detective called New York, got all the clues, figured out who the killer was, and had someone make the arrest. That has to take place on stage or the reader will feel cheated and will not walk with us again. Nor will an editor or agent pick up our work to begin with.

I know of a writer who, in a story, brought a plane in for a crash landing, almost out of gas, and ended the chapter as it was ready to touch down. Okay so far. But three chapters later when he picked up at this thread again, the characters were in a coffee shop talking about what a narrow escape it had been.

That's a no no.

After building towards a climax, we owe it to our readers to show them how it played out.

Reading Aloud

One of the greatest tools we have in rewriting is to read aloud. If we can't read a sentence out loud, there is something wrong with it. We either need to reword it, add punctuation, or break it apart. This is obvious in dialogue, but equally important in narrative. If something doesn't sound right, it won't read right.

Reading out loud will also point out the rough spots, the cadence of repetitious sentences, words missing or used repeatedly. Phrases creep into our writing like they do in conversation, and if we keep repeating them they will detract from our story.

In *The Matarese Countdown*, Robert Ludlum used "you know that" and "young man" so much in dialogue I ended up tossing the book across the room. You and I, without a big name, would never get away with it.

Reading into a tape recorder and playing it back will do all of the above plus give us an ear for our dialogue. Does it sound logical? Do all the characters sound alike? Have we sufficiently identified who is talking, either in dialogue or internal monologue? It's also a good way to tune our ear to our writing voice. This is the way our readers will hear our writing. Are we too harsh, too cute, right on? And it will give us an idea of how our writing will sound if it is ever made into an audio book; something to think about.

Reading our work aloud, or into a tape recorder, or having someone else read it to us will improve our writing and storytelling. Is it more work? Yes. Is it time consuming? Yes. But considering the odds we are up against in getting our work looked at by agents and editors, doesn't it make sense to use every tool at our disposal?

Would you build a house with rusty nails?

Voice

We're talking about narrative voice here, and I guess this is as good a time as any to describe it.

But Voice is elusive. Someone described it as, "I don't know what it is, but when you find it, you'll know it."

So how do I tell you about something like that?

I think it's a bit like talking on a telephone or making a speech into a microphone. We use a different voice when we do that. To give you an example, I have a friend who stutters, sometimes to the point I want to help him finish his sentences, but when he gets on the telephone it all immediately drops away and he doesn't skip a beat.

I think Voice cuts in when we evolve from trying to *write*, like it's this magnificent thing that will impress the world, and start to relate our story, in conversational tone, as if our readers are listening to us across the kitchen table. Sometimes it helps to picture a reader, preferably a stranger so we have to make everything clear. I think it only comes after a lot of writing. For some it's light and flowing, others humorous, others serious, and maybe even heavy.

The good thing is, once we find it, we have it for all time, although I often find that when I'm into a new novel, it might be somewhere in the middle before it kicks in. When it does, I know it immediately. The vague feeling that something was missing suddenly snaps into place and I have the confidence that it's probably going to work out.

This all sounds nebulous, but I think that's what Voice is. We can pick it up in good books, something that sounds right to us, like we are hearing the author. But trying to describe it is like trying to describe the ocean from a bucket of water.

I think if we work at relating our story the best we can to our imaginary reader across the table, somewhere along the way we'll find our Voice. Or maybe, it's the other way around; our Voice will find us.

Hard Copy

Sooner or later we'll have to print out a hard copy if we hope to send it to an agent/editor. So, remember when I said back in chapter two that printed words look different than written words? Well, folks, hard-copy words look different than computer monitor words. Rough spots that slipped by staring at the tube now stand out like red painted gargoyles. Things we had honed to a sharp edge now appear dull and lifeless. Don't ask me why, they just do. Every writer I know says the same thing. I think it has to do with format.

Someone recently told me they get around it by e-mailing a chapter to themselves, and just seeing it in a different format is enough to pop out the same errors they normally see on a hard copy.

Well, that sounded like a good idea to me, so I used one of the pages on my web site and transferred a chapter onto it using

Netscape Composer. Bingo. All the same things that caught my eye on a hard copy, caught my eye on the HTML page. The width of the page was narrower, the background color was different, and I think that was enough of a change to cast the writing in another light.

Just be aware that once we've either transferred our final writing into a different format, or printed out a hard copy, we'll have to run through our novel one more time to make these, hopefully, last changes.

A writer must hold nothing back. He must write as if the novel is the last he will write in his life.

—V.S. Naipaul

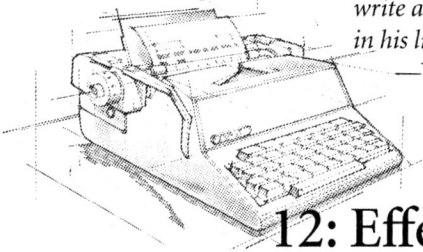

12: Effective Writing Concluded

Worn Out Words

Clichés are like passive sentences in that they rob our work of spontaneity. New writers pull up clichés and think they're being right in the swing, but for me, been there, done that.

All phrases in public conversation were at one time fresh and pleasant to the ears, but thanks to television commercials beating a dead horse, it all gets to feel like, been there, done that by the time it gets into print.

The only thing worse is putting the cliché in quotes.

> Thanks to television commercials beating a "dead horse," it all gets to feel like "been there, done that" by the time it gets into print.

This is like shouting, "Look, look, hackneyed writing."

We use these things in conversational speech all the time without realizing it, which brings up the one place where we can use them, in dialogue.

> "Hey, girl, I have a blind date tonight."
> "Oh God, chile, been there, done that."

There are other worn out words that should be treated as suspect because they don't mean anything specific.

very
nice
real
really
true
truly
awesome

And there are other words that in most cases should be thrown out.

almost
seemed
seemingly
somehow

In "almost" every sentence these words appear you can leave them out without changing the meaning.

> He did it seemingly without effort. Later I learned how much it taxed him.

Suppose we left out seemingly? Does it not read the same? If we are the observer, he did it without effort.

But the one I hate the most is "somehow."

Somehow she knew someone was behind her.

Bullshit.

What a lazy way of writing.

Give me something, the reek of cigarettes, the feeling of a presence, or even just leave the word out. And yet we see it all the time. *All* the time.

Along with these nothing words we allow nothing phrases to creep into our work. "As you know…" If we already know it, do we have to say it? That's as bad as "It goes without saying…" which started the chapter on effective writing. There are also redundant phrases that are used too often, like "a dead body…" which I see a lot in mysteries.

Other cliché phrases I see all the time:

She challenged him with her eyes.
She fixed a menacing look on George.
Misery was stamped on his face.
Her face had a look of pure horror.
Her eyes opened in horror.
Her eyes twinkled.
Sidney was all ears.
Jane said it all with her expression.
She made a face—she pulled a face.

Can we actually see any of these things? I can't see horror in someone eyes, but if her eyes bulged and her mouth opened in a silent scream, that I can see. And what is making a face or pulling a face? Is it a grimace? Then why not say grimace? Crossed her eyes and stuck out her tongue? Is it a snarl, eyebrows raised in a question, brows knitted in anger? Why not just describe what we mean rather than the easy cliché, she pulled a face?

We have to keep these wordmongers from creeping into our work.

Abresch's Order of Rewriting

This is the way I normally put a novel together. You might use it for a starting model, but I want to emphasize this is *my* way, because my way might not work for you. You might find it's better for you to rewrite as you go along. And some writers can't stand the thought of going through from beginning to end on successive drafts and rewrite chapter by chapter. All of this is subjective.

During the first draft the driving force is to get it finished, keeping notes on characters and things I need to go back and change. If I see a paragraph that might need changing, I might do it, but the driving force is not to get bogged down. Get it done.

Once this is completed I go through a fast and dirty second draft. I'll try to smooth some things now, but the main thrust is to straighten out all the things I made notes to change while I went through the first draft. If I changed someone's name in chapter thirty, or added a new character, changed a location or stabbed someone, I have to go back and reflect this in earlier chapters. We'll take up foreshadowing in more detail in chapter twenty-two.

Then I do character profiles using notes I've made as I wrote the first draft. When I finish these, enough time will have gone by so I can look at the novel with a fresh approach.

On the third draft I'll be at greater pains to smooth the writing out, but I'll concentrate more on getting the characters right, what clothes they're wearing. At this time I'll also work on descriptions, the weather, noise and smells, whatever is needed to give a sense of place. "He drove *through the cold, rainy afternoon* to Sally's house." Spending those five italicized words can do a lot to put our reader in the picture. I track the weather changes as the story moves along. Still, knowing I have at least one more draft gives me permission to continue working on character and place even though I might not be absolutely satisfied with the writing.

In the fourth draft I am again trying to smooth the writing, but the main thrust here is consistency. I do this by breaking out each character and tracking him/her through the story, reading only the parts where that character appears, making sure there is consistency in body language, dialogue, background, and actions. If I have some business built into the story, I might yank that out as well, checking it for redundancy and to make sure it all hangs together.

Finally, in the last draft, I put all my effort into trying to smooth out the writing so one sentence leads into another, one paragraph leads into another, so there are no stumbling blocks in the road. I'll also be working from either a hard copy or from an HTML format at this time.

Then, hopefully, I'm ready to ship it off to find out what my editor wants me to change.

Conclusion

If you're getting a steady stream of rejections, perhaps you're sending in work a few drafts too soon. If we learn from these examples—specifics for generalities; active voice for passive; and reaching for the right words, nouns and verbs, rather than accepting adjectives and adverbs and hackneyed clichés—then we'll end up far down the road to effective writing.

You can't do it on the cheap.

Have I said this before?

When we have completed all our rewriting and we're getting ready for submission, now is the time to run some last minute checks.

Do a search on "ly" for adverbs and adjectives that might be robbing our story of more powerful verbs and nouns.

Do a search on *that*, which often creeps into our work, and eliminate those that are unnecessary.

If there is a personal error you continue to make, like for me it's using "it's" for "its," do a search for these and clear them up.

All of these seem picky problems when what we want to do is get the story out there, but in this world of bottom-line profits, editors and agents will toss stories that are full of misspellings and grammatical errors.

An on-line writer friend of mine, Harry Arnston, who helped me a lot and has since passed away, always advocated, "give them no reason to reject your work."

That's what we face in trying to get published—not giving them a reason to reject our work. We don't have a big name. We haven't yet built up a readership. We can't hope that a great plot will get us by. Or good characters. Or fantastic writing. We need it all. We have to take up the challenge and write so that we dare those who judge our work to put it down.

Whew.

This brings us to the end of effective writing/rewriting. The subject, like plot and characterization, is interwoven and interlaced with everything else, description, dialogue, narration, point of view, but this gives us an idea of some of the things to look for in working our way from that terrible first draft to our tight, crisp, dare-them-to-put-it-down manuscript.

Writing is like prostitution. First you do it for love, and then for a few close friends, and then for money.
—Moliere

13: Head with a View

POV

Point of View, or POV in writer's shorthand, is the reference character through whom we are witnessing our story. Like we are in their head, privy to their thoughts, peering out their eyeballs.

> I went to the beach and the waves were so high I thought I would die. They would swamp me. No way was I going into that water.

This POV is a conversational narrative of what happened on a woman's vacation. We see not only what she saw but we're also privy to her thoughts, which color everything we hear. This is a First Person POV, and in using it we reveal the world to our readers through First Person's head.

> She went to the beach and saw the big waves. Oh no. They would swamp her. No way was she going into the water.

This is Third Person Subjective POV, meaning we are in Third Person's head. We know her thoughts. Everything's about the same, except for the pronouns.

> They went to the beach and saw the big waves. Marsha shuddered at the idea of getting in among them, but John smiled at the thought of skimming along on his surfboard.

This tells the story in Omniscient POV, meaning that, like God, we can see into everyone's head at the same time. Using this POV we allow the reader to know all pertinent thoughts the characters have within a scene.

> Marsha and John went to the beach. Big waves crashed onto the shore. Marsha's eyes opened wide and her jaw dropped. John smiled and rubbed the palms of his hands together.

This is Narrative POV, meaning we are in the narrator's head and seeing only what Narrator sees. All character thoughts are surmised from actions and body language. We could also make the Narrator a First Person, a character telling the story about other people.

We can also mix and match, but this becomes very tricky and we could end up confusing our readers. It might make a good experiment, but editors seldom buy experimental first novels.

So, let's look at them more closely.

First and Second Person POV

The advantages of using a First Person POV is that readers see and feel everything as First Person sees and feels it. Also, by using the "I" and "me" pronouns the reader personally picks up on it, becoming the "I" of the story, which brings about the maximum character identification. Many beginning writers choose this POV because it is the way they would normally relate something to a friend.

The disadvantages are the same things. If our protagonist is a murderer or a rapist, First Person may bring about more identification with the character than our readers want. Also, since First Person is the narrator, the reader knows she will probably be alive at story's end. Not a problem for mystery series where we know the hero will still be around, but it might take a slight edge off if we want to keep the protagonist's fate in doubt.

The advantage of Third Person is we can maintain that doubt about the protagonist's fate until the end. Also, Third Person is just a shade less in character identification than First Person, but it is enough to allow a repulsive protagonist without the reader feeling uncomfortable. A beginning writer may feel less at ease in Third Person than First Person. My old college professor recommended writing in First Person and then changing all the "I's" to "she's" or "he's." It works as a learning tool, but the conversion is not quite that simple.

The advantages and disadvantages that apply to both First and Third Person POVs are that the writer is limited to only what POV sees and feels. POV cannot view something across town or off-camera. And we must *never* keep relevant POV knowledge from our reader or they will feel cheated.

For instance, we can't have a First/Third person POV detective in a mystery suddenly jump up at the end and shout, "I have found the killer, and it is me." That's obvious. If the detective knew he did it, so would the reader inside his head. But it applies as well to something less obvious like:

> I made secret plans to trap the killer, but in order to keep it from the reader, I blanked out my mind while I thought about it.

Oh, yeah.

Substitute "he" for "I" and it doesn't help. If POV sees it and thinks it, we who are wallowing around in POV's head have to see and know it as well.

One of the big mistakes a new writer makes is stating another's feelings, like assuming POV can read another character's mind.

> Oself looked at Sally. Sally thought he smelled bad and didn't like him. Oself was disappointed because he liked her.

There is no way Oself's POV could know what Sally was thinking. We might try to dramatize it, but we would not know if the interpretation was correct:

> Oself looked at Sally. Her nose wrinkled up whenever he came near her and she acted like she couldn't wait to get away. That was disappointing. Oself liked her.

The thing to remember is to stay inside POV's head.

Can we ever come out of POV?

Not First Person. We can never say, "I ate subconsciously." If I say it I am obviously aware of what I'm doing, and vice versa.

I think we can more easily switch from Third Person Subjective to Objective for a few paragraphs, say to describe the POV character. If it's done skillfully, the reader will not be aware of it. Like everything else, folks, you can get away with anything if it's done with great skill. For the rest of us, it is by far better to remain within POV at all times.

A good example of how to handle POV is Linda Barnes's *Carlotta Carlyle* mystery series. Worth a look.

Using a single POV, First or Third Person, will bring about a closer reader identification and a faster read than anything else. As POV experiences his/her ups and downs, doubts and fears, joys and sorrows, so will the reader. It's seamless in that there are no shifts for our readers to disengage from one POV mind and enter another.

Multiple POVs are the same as Third Person POV, except that we shift heads, or POV character, from scene to scene. This is probably the most used POV of all so we'll devote the next chapter to it.

Narrative POV

We said that in First and Third Person POV we see what POV sees and when he sees it. We can't know what's happening across town, or what other people are saying about him when he is not present.

One way around this is to have a First/Third Person POV who is not the protagonist. We have instead a narrator objectively tell the story of the protagonist. Now the narrator can know everything that's happening around the protagonist, know what other people say and think about him/her, and what's happening across town. This is very much like a movie with the camera as the narrator.

We can even make the narrator subjective, that is, a POV character relating his/her feelings about the protagonist. This is not the choice many writers make, and I wouldn't recommend it for a beginner, but it's done well by John Le Carré in *Russia House*. Worth a look.

The same POV limitations apply. Narrator cannot know what others are thinking, but only show their thoughts through their actions.

Omniscient POV

Now we can know all things about all people all the time.

In Omniscient POV we are like God, seeing and relating what's in everyone's head within the scene. At first blush this might sound like the way to go. We can move everyone along at the same time, knowing immediately if someone hates another, knowing all the snide remarks each person is making inside their heads, and it's a bit like a movie scene as well, except in a movie we can't know what's going on in a person's head.

I think the disadvantages outweigh the advantages.

It's hard to capture reader identification. Because we are bombarded with character thoughts from all over, there is less to bind the reader to a single character's fate. If we want to build a series around a hero, this would be the last way to go.

The other disadvantage is that we can't hide relevant thoughts of *anybody* while in a scene. This can lessen whatever suspense we are trying to create. If John was determined to kill Marsha from the beginning of the book, and the reader, despite knowing John's other thoughts, doesn't know about that until the end, he/she is going to feel cheated.

I think this is the most difficult POV to master, and yet beginners jump into it because of the apparent advantages. I've read some good books using Omniscient POV, but I don't believe I was ever as deeply engaged as in books with First/Third person POVs. Just my opinion.

Internal Monologue

In Subjective First, Third, or Multiple POVs, we place the reader inside the POV's head. We do that through narration and internal dialogue. If we do it well, the switch from one to the other is imperceptible.

> I watched him thread the fishing line through the eye of the hook. I thought to myself, how well he does this with one hand.

Notice how this goes from narrative to thought, but is it imperceptible? "I thought to myself"? Duh. Who else you going to think to? But leave out all the thinking:

> I watched him thread the fishing line through the eye of the hook. How well he does this with one hand.

There is no ambiguity here. Only First Person could be thinking that second sentence. It works equally well in Third.

> He stared at the miniature tree, peeled end pointed at him like a stick.
>
> So what was this, a joke?
>
> He shifted to the wild eyes glaring back at him.
>
> Was the guy going stab him with a three-foot bonsai tree?

Notice the shift from the first and third sentence narrative to the second and forth sentence internal dialogue. We don't have to say, "he thought," and in fact "he thought" would be intrusive, as if we need to instruct readers. I maintain that in handling Subjective POV well, we never have to say, "he/she thought." Worse yet would be to put it in italics. Long passages in italics are intrusive. Readers don't like reading them.

Even in Omniscient POV you can get away without using "thought" by juxtaposing some action or identifier just before the internal monologue:

> "Ah," Harry said, "why would women think you're handsome?" This guy was a conceited fool, what with his square jaw and olive skin.
>
> "I didn't say they did," John said and shrugged. Maybe not handsome, but from the look in women's eyes there was no doubt he had plucked a few heart strings.

By linking interior monologue to an action, dialogue, or tag we can identify who is doing the thinking:

> I debated whether to tell her, then shrugged. "I had to kill him."
>
> Sally was filled with horror.

How does First Person know Sally is filled with horror? A First or Third Person Subjective POV cannot know what's in another person's head. If POV can read a person's mind one time, why not all people all the time? And what does "filled with horror," show us anyway? Go back and check out clichés. Let's redo it and add a third sentence.

> I debated whether to tell her, then shrugged. "I had to kill him."
>
> Sally's eyes opened wide, jaw clenched so tight it dimpled her chin as she drew back from me.
>
> I must horrify her.

Now we can see Sally's reaction rather then being told, and First Person's interpretation of it, which always leaves a question because it could be wrong. This limitation is also an advantage. An argument, a bit of humor, a dangerous situation can all be brought about by the protagonist misinterpreting another's action.

When we dramatize what is happening, we engage the reader, yet too many times writers will settle for the fast cliché, or tell us what to feel. It's easier than using the imagination. Or maybe it's because, consciously or not, they don't trust their readers. What's even worse is to show it and then tell it.

> "You disgust me," she said with revulsion.

This sort of writing will wear over the course of a novel, producing a less satisfying and slower read, and will likely garner negative notice from agents and editors.

The corollary also holds true. While First/Third Person Subjective POV cannot know what another character is thinking, we must always let the reader know what POV is thinking. If our POV knows pertinent facts and hides them till the end, the reader is going to feel cheated.

Stuart Kaminsky, whose writing I like, wove a marvelous First Person yarn in *A Fatal Glass of Beer*, but at the end First Person makes a plan without telling the reader what it is. Something like he called his friend and told him his plan. Kaminsky did it to heighten the reader's suspense and enjoyment of the finale, but I think it would have been a less obvious device to know the plan and wrap the suspense around its possible failure. It's a minor point in an otherwise good story, and had I not been reading as a writer, to learn as well as enjoy, I might not have picked up on it.

When a device becomes obvious, it's intrusive. When it's intrusive, it impedes story flow like a rock in a brook, and if it's flagrant our readers end up giving us a bye.

Do we want our readers to come and journey with us again?

An advantage of Multiple POV is not being stuck with the same character all the time.

—Lawrence Block at the Washington Independent Writers Spring Conference

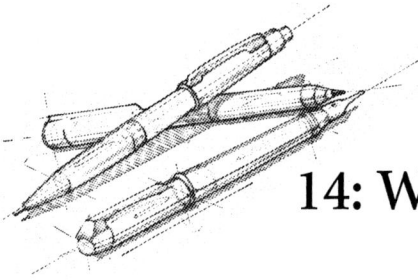

14: Whose Eyeballs?

Multiple POVs

Another way around the limitations placed on Third Person POV is to have Multiple POVs. This is different from Omniscient POV in that we maintain the rule of being inside only one head; we just switch heads as we move through the story. Sort of like changing horses on the trail. Just remember, we can only ride one horse at a time.

If Oself is a CIA agent tracking down plutonium, and we want to show our readers that a woman KGB agent is assigned the same task, we can do it through shifting POVs to show the woman agent being assigned the same task. Then we can bounce back and forth between the heads of the two agents, and perhaps others, as we move through the story. This, done well, can bring about tension, for the reader knows the trouble that both Oself and the woman agent are walking into. A great example of Multiple POV is *The Day of the Jackal* by Frederick Forsyth. Everyone knows the killer does not bump off de Gaulle, and yet, Forsyth maintains the tension that locks us in until the end. Another good example is Stuart Kaminsky's *Tarnished Icons*.

Multiple POVs allow us to let the reader in on part of the story that the protagonist doesn't know.

POV Shifts

Our grip on our readers is weakest when we make a POV shift.

They have been comfortably traveling along in one POV's head, getting to know and bond with him/her, then suddenly—pop—they're in a new head. They have nothing invested in this new POV. It's a good time for them to put down the book and turn out the light. Because of this it is essential to hook our readers into the first paragraph, give them something so when they turn off that light they'll be anxious to get back the following day.

And since reader interest flags during POV shifts, we should limit them to those that are absolutely necessary to tell the story. Try long scenes or a whole chapter in each POV rather than chopping them up into five shifts in two pages.

In the same way we need to limit our POV characters. In a big war epoch this number could be high, but even here we should investigate ways of combining actions and scenes to eliminate POVs. We touched on this in storyboarding.

Finally, we need to make sure our readers know when a POV shift has taken place and who the new POV is, preferably in the first paragraph. The more POV shifts we make and the more POV characters we have, the more likely we'll confuse our readers. Confuse 'em and lose 'em, folks.

In addition to letting the reader know who the new POV character is, we need to create a tag, an action, or a bit of business to tie that POV character back into the reader's mind. Four chapters may have gone by since our readers last saw this guy on stage, and even mentioning his name might not be a big wow.

Who is this joker?

But if we've shown him owning a prized Jaguar in a previous chapter and in the new POV shift he gets out of that car, bingo, we're back in. If a woman had been previously flirting with a man and we shift her back in to show her on a date with that guy, we know who she is. Or if he has been concerned about losing his hair and in the shift we see him combing his hair around to cover up the bald spot, we've tagged him.

The cardinal sin in POV shifts, or in bringing anyone back on stage for that matter, is to do such a poor job that our readers must thumb back through the book to find out who the character is. This is a drop dead stop in the flow of our story. We can't take it for granted that just because a reader started our book that they'll finish it. And even if they do, will they be so enthralled that they'll come back and travel with us again? We're not talking about a single-book career, folks, we're talking about building a readership that will journey on with us, and will get their friends to climb aboard as well.

Switching POVs is similar to ending a chapter. If we do it at a dramatic point, the reader will be anxious to pick up on that POV when he/she shows up again. That works up to a point. While I like Elmore Leonard's writing, like *Moonshine War*, *Bandits*, and *Swag*, the end of *Maximum Bob* had so many shifts in the middle of an action that I wanted to trash the book. The device had become obvious and therefore intrusive and annoying when all I wanted to do was get on with the story.

Dangers of Multiple POVs

Wow, that sounds ominous. Like someone's going to kill us if we get it wrong? Well, we could by killing our story's chances if we screw it up.

We said our readers want to experience another life, one that is more exciting, less lonely, more romantic. We help them to do that by giving them a character to identify with, someone to call their own for the story's journey. Remember Oself, our other self?

When a reader opens a book and reads the first few lines, this is a contract between writer and reader of what the book is about. Our readers will assume the first POV is that of the protagonist, our Oself character. Unless there is an overriding reason for not doing so, I suggest we make the protagonist the first POV. There are ways around this. Open with a prologue or strictly narration. This will prevent confusion on the reader's part when the protagonist finally steps on stage.

Also, if we dilute our Multiple POVs too thin, we stand the chance of completely losing any reader identification.

In *Total Control*, David Baldacci commits both these sins, starting off with a minor character POV and then shifting POVs in equal measure so that I never could figure out who the protagonist was. I kept waiting for someone to step forward and take—forgive me—total control. All of which made the book a difficult read for me.

Once again, the main reason for shifting POVs is to let our readers in on part of the story a single POV could not know. We can have a shift from Oself to George and inside George's head we find out something that Oself doesn't know. Then we can switch back into Oself's head and our readers' suspense is heightened because they know what's awaiting Oself down the road.

The danger here is if we reveal things to our readers that should be obvious to Oself, and Oself doesn't get it, we could end up making Oself look stupid. If we develop a super-smart lawyer as a character and then have her make a zillion stupid mistakes, we could end up with our readers rooting for the killer to blow her brains out. It's hard to identify with a dolt. The caution should always be: is Oself's lack of awareness logical, or because it's better for the plot?

For instance, if Oself is looking for a murder weapon, and in a POV shift the villain hides a chef's knife behind some books in the library, fine, there is no way Oself could know that. But if Villain sets it in the middle of the desk, still dripping blood, and Oself doesn't notice, we begin to wonder how swift he is. It might work for plot, but not for logic. Even worse is if Oself picks up the knife while glancing around the room. This elbow-in-the-ribs joke is so obvious we lose credibility.

But what if the weapon is a steel ruler? This might work because the ruler belongs on a desk and it's not an obvious weapon. Oself might even pick it up, but we need finesse now because we're on the edge between a serious scene and a cliché guffaw. Of course, if the guffaw is what we want, then cliché works.

We also have to be careful we don't build up so many things the reader knows, and Oself doesn't, that reader frustration sets in. I've read books where things are piled so high I wanted to shout to the protagonist to open his eyes and get on with it. Maybe part of it had to do with things that should have been obvious to Oself and weren't, and maybe part of it was the writer used the device so much it became intrusive. Over-egged the custard, as the British say.

Anything done well and with finesse will work. Treat it with a heavy hand and it will crash down around us.

One final bit of advice for Multiple POVs.

All POVs must be consistent, just like characters. The way they speak and dress and think is dependent on their background. So somewhere between the second and final draft, break out all the sections for each POV and read them consecutively as if each POV is a separate novel. Does the POV maintain consistency in narrative voice, internal monologue, actions, and goals? If not, resolve it. Does each POV sound different than the other POVs? If not, resolve that as well. This also works when we get to dialogue.

My own feeling, mentioned before, is that using a single First or Third Person POV will bring about a closer reader identification and a faster, easier read than anything else. However, too many writers have been successful in using Multiple POVs for us to dismiss it as a lesser method. Just watch out for Multiple POV's multiple booby traps along the way.

When we bring our readers into the heads of our characters, we wrap the reader tightly into our story and dare them to put it down. This, by its very nature, will give a faster, easier read. Do it well.

> *Don't say the old lady screamed. Bring her on and let her scream.*
> —Mark Twain

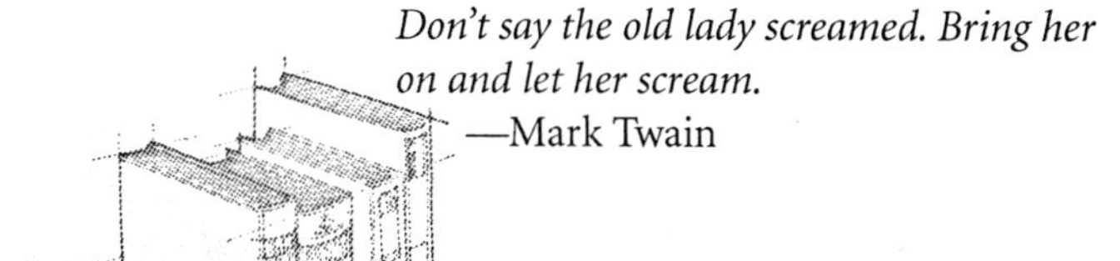

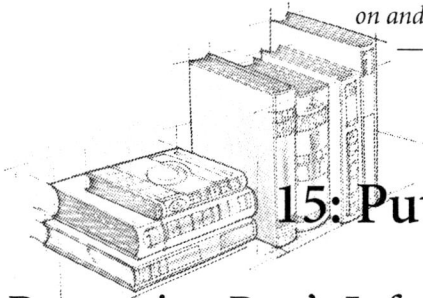

15: Put Them on Stage

Dramatize, Don't Inform

Most people call this, "show, don't tell." Since this has become a writing cliché, some people have called it "display, don't tell." Now you may think I'm gilding the lily by using "dramatize, don't inform," but this is the kernel of what we're seeking.

Why am I telling you this?

Because there's a fine line between showing and telling, and sometimes it disappears completely.

> The room was dark with the one light over the bar half hidden by cigarette smoke.

That's showing us, and telling us. It's also informing us, but is it drama? If the description above were of a scene on stage, we would call it backdrop. Or props. Settings. But the drama, that's what's taking place between the actors. We could make it more dramatic:

> The room was dark with the bar light gauzed over by an acrid cloud of cigarette smoke.

But it's still not drama.

> Oself entered the dark room and cut his way through the acrid soup of cigarette smoke that stung his nostrils, turned his stomach, and damn near clouded out the one light over the bar. He sat down and ordered a drink.

Now we have drama. Maybe over-drama. What's the difference? The first two are informing us of what is. The third shows, or dramatizes, Oself's reaction on entering the room. Everything is seen, tasted, smelled, felt through his viewpoint.

The thing is, folks, do we want to spend these extra words to dramatize it? We could just say:

> The room was dark with one light over the bar half hidden by cigarette smoke.
>
> Oself sat down and ordered a drink.

That works, doesn't it? With a lot less words.

So back to the question, do we spend the words or not?

It depends on what we are trying to do. If it is important to show the reader what the bar was like, or if an action takes place there, or we need to show how Oself felt, I'd probably spend the words. But if just a quick stop to pick up information from a bartender, I might save them.

Probably and might?

Wow, that's definitive.

The thing is, it's the author's call. There are times when we have to inform. But since the majority of our novels need to be dramatized, all actions and interactions, we need to be sure what we're talking about.

Dramatize, not inform, gilding the lily or not, the advice holds. In spades.

> The woman watched. The man was mysterious and had contempt written on his face as he passed a boy with his hat out. The little boy was so forlorn that her heart went out to him. Such a sad little boy. The world had treated him harshly. She was miserable for him and in a rage that the man passed him by.

What have we dramatized here? Does "mysterious" pop an image into our mind? And I'm glad contempt is written on the man's face, hopefully in red letters, otherwise would we see it? Can we see forlorn, or feel her heart go out to him? Maybe he's sad and been treated harshly, but we only know it because we've been *informed*. Can we see she's miserable or in a rage, or is there even enough to trigger such a POV reaction? Since it is superficial and full of generalities, it doesn't engage our senses, and therefore creates no response in us.

I think that is the key.

Does it elicit a response?

Okay, I exaggerated the example, but how to solve it?

First of all we need to bring our actors on stage.

In the writing of so many beginners I see one person on stage flatly telling us what has happened, what is happening, what is going to happen. If you shelled out big bucks to see a play, would you want to sit in the audience and watch this for three acts?

Next, because this isn't a play but a novel, we need to have a POV, someone the reader can identify with. Since it is the woman who is watching and reacting to everything, she's the POV. To make her more personal for reader identification, we'll give her a name.

> Amy watched a man stride along with a black hat pulled down over his brow, dark eyes shifting about as if he were hiding from someone. A boy, maybe five years old, raised an upturned cap at the man's approached, eyes wide in his scrubbed face.
>
> "Some bread for my sick mother, sir."
>
> The man's lips curled and he spit on the ground as he passed by.
>
> Amy stared after him.
>
> He didn't have to do that. She wanted to shout after him, but instead shifted back to the boy.
>
> Everything drooped: his head of soft brown hair; shoulders in a thin, brown jacket; hands at his sides three inches below the cuffs. He lifted his head at an approaching couple, a smile on the little face, eyebrows raised, but the smile faded and the eyebrows fell as the couple swept by before he could utter his piece.
>
> Amy stared at him a moment, then stood up, crossed over, and dropped five coppers in the cap.

All right, now we have the actors on stage and the action unfolds before us.

We don't have to be told the man is mysterious, the black hat over his brow and dark shifting eyes give us that, and combined with the striding along gives us an action picture of him. The "as if he had something to hide" is okay because it's Amy's interpretation if what she sees.

We don't have to be *informed* the little boy is forlorn and sad, we can *see* it in his clothes and actions; we don't have to be told of his desolation because we can feel it. Seeing all that, do we question Amy's action of dropping five coppers in his cap?

Doesn't this also tell us something about Amy?

It does spend a lot more words, but look what we are getting for our money. We plop ourselves down in the scene and watch it unfold about us. A scene can't be experienced in narrative summation or telling. It only happens when we make it immediate by dramatizing it.

Two more things.

First, in our corrected example, we could have added a sentence before dropping the coppers in the cap.

> Amy stared at him a moment. *What a forlorn waif he was.* She stood up, crossed over, and dropped five coppers in the cap.

Now we can get away with the forlorn bit because it is Amy's reaction to the picture we've shown. Instead of informing us what we should feel, it's now showing us what Amy feels.

Second, we could add another sentence and a few words to completely change the focus and mood.

> Everything drooped: his head of soft brown hair; shoulders in a thin, brown

> jacket; hands at his sides three inches below the cuffs. *He turned his bowed head to steal a glance at the retreating man, sneered, and threw him an obscene gesture.*

With that one sentence we've changed our little boy from a forlorn waif in need of a handout, to a street-wise opportunist. All it takes is a little drama.

Of course, if I were really doing this, I would add some props—a park bench, trees, sidewalk and snow, an icy wind to feel and maybe a nearby bakery with bread to smell.

> Amy rested on a park bench. Snow still covered the walk from a recent storm. An icy wind whistled through the bare branches of Linden trees and brought with it the smell of bread from a nearby bakery.
>
> She watched a man stride along…

But notice this new paragraph informs us as much as it shows us. We could dramatize it by spending more words to show Amy shivering and her mouth watering at the smell of bread, but that's not the real drama here. The drama is what's happening to the boy and her reaction to that, so probably we would not want to spend the extra words.

Okay, okay, okay, okay.

What the hell is Amy doing resting on a snow-covered bench?

I don't know.

Ask her.

Originally I had the boy's "eyebrows raised in hope" and also "eyebrows fell in a forlorn flicker" in the next to last sentence, but I took it out because it was not only telling, but the scene is stronger without it. Over-telling something actually makes it weaker. We present the picture and respect our reader's intelligence to come up with the right conclusion.

> "Are you coming?"
>
> Marsha said it all with her negative expression. "I am not going with you."
>
> He stormed out of the house.

Can we see a negative expression? I can see a shaking of the head, but that's not what it says. And if she *said* it all with her expression, do we need to say it again in the dialogue? Isn't this a bit like telling our readers they're are too dumb to get the dialogue without the instructions? How about if we showed it?

> "Are you coming?"
>
> Marsha glanced at the ceiling, then closed her eyes and shook her head. "I am not going with you."
>
> He stormed out of the house.

We can see that now. Perhaps it triggers a response of disgust or exaggerated patience. It dramatizes how Marsha feels, which we now reinforce with the dialogue, but we could also have dropped the dialogue and let it stand alone.

I glanced at a romance novel at an airport newsstand recently. The story opened with a woman answering the doorbell past midnight, in nightgown and bathrobe, bare feet and mussed hair. Doesn't this present us with a complete picture? Yet, the author felt compelled to say, "it was obvious from her gown and robe and bare feet that he had gotten her out of bed." Duh. If that's my reaction, doesn't it stop the story? And might I not put down the book and walk away? I might, and did.

Let's take a look at a few more examples:

> She challenged George with her eyes.

Can we see that? What does it look like?

But how about:

> She glared at him, tight jaw working so it popped out tiny muscles in her cheeks.

Do we have to be told how this lady is feeling? Our readers know anger when they see it. And if you want something less, just have her glare at him.

> Jace was agitated and his eyes were filled with pure horror.

The eyes filled with horror gets me; it's a hackneyed phrase that shows us nothing, and filled with "pure" horror tells us even less, yet I see all the time. Compare it with this from Beth Amos's *Eyes of Night.*

> Jace finally responded, his eyes shifting toward Kerri's. But the tongue kept patrolling the inside of his mouth…

Can't we see Jace's agitation from that vivid picture? If she were to add, "Jace was agitated," it would only detract from the description. It would be like saying her readers are so stupid they need to be told what it means.

When we write an action scene, character reactions and motions and body language, imagine it on a stage or in a movie. Can we see what's happening from our words? If not, we're informing. In fact, watching a television show or a video with the sound turned off would be a good learning aid. Watch how the camera shows us what is taking place. It is the eyes of our POV character. What we have to do is convert it into words and then boil it down to the very essence of what we are trying to convey.

Informing instead of dramatizing is so insidious, and easy to do, we have to constantly guard against it. Me too. If you find some informing-instead-of-dramatizing in my work, know that I'm the first to admit I have clay feet. Size nine. But it all takes away from engaging our readers. When we show-instead-of-tell it well, our readers aren't even aware of us or our words, but only what is unfolding before them in their dream.

Inform Instead of Dramatize

Say what?

After all this dramatize-not-inform business, now we're supposed to inform?

When we need to convey information our readers need to know, but is only peripheral to the story—things that happen off-stage; retelling events our readers already know; indicate passage of time; or to execute scene transitions—it's better to do it fast and dirty in narrative summation which is…informing. Or telling.

> Oself and Sally left Margaret's house. They got into the taxi. Outside the windows the city passed by. The taxi stopped

> for a red light. When it turned green again, they moved on. More buildings passed by. The driver hurried through a yellow light before it turned red. He missed the turn to George's street and had to circle the block. They finally arrived. Oself got out and paid the driver. They went up the stairs to find Bob waiting for them.

This is dramatizing it, in a minimal way, but unless there is a story reason for showing the scenery, or an action in the taxi, it's also bor-ring. We can cut this out by informing and we don't even have to say how they traveled.

> Oself and Sally left Margaret's. When they got to George's house they found Bob waiting for them.

This goes equally well for a passage of time. Instead of leaves falling, headlines changing, clocks spinning forward, all we need is, "Six months later..." This should be obvious, but sometimes we overlook the obvious.

What might not be so obvious is retelling something we've already shown.

Say we have an accident scene involving our Oself character and we show that scene. A couple of chapters later a detective shows up and wants to know what happened. Well, the obvious thing is to tell the detective everything so he will know what happened. The thing is, folks, our readers already know what happened. So rather than bore them with pages of dialogue, we inform them with a simple narrative summation.

> Oself told the detective about the accident.

Suppose there were some plot points there that we want to reiterate to remind our readers?

> Oself told the detective about the accident, including plot point one and plot point two.

There are also times we need to convey information so our readers will understand what's going on: native customs; a bit of history; background action in a war; technical details; but stopping the action to tell anything is intrusive. If there's no way around it, there's no way around it.

Let's go back to our stage analogy.

Do we want to sit out there while an actor goes on and on in a stage aside? That's the problem we're facing. So what we have to do is make the information concise and interesting. It will not solve the problem, but if we do it later in the story, not right at the beginning, it will make it tolerable.

We can also alleviate it by breaking it up.

Join the information with an action. As we watch someone climbing a mountain we can intersperse the action with the mountain's history. The same thing for a battle.

We can also intersperse information with conversation. Or try filtering it through dialogue when it would be natural for characters to discuss it. The caution here is that if we have dialogue only to inform our readers, they will spot it immediately as unnatural.

Suppose we need character background? Rather than have a long exposition, tell it in snippets when it's needed. Or better yet, dramatize it in a flashback.

Suppose we need a technical point explained. Rather than stop the action, try to bring a no-knowledge character on-stage to ask about it. This allows our Oself character to give an over-simplified explanation to his no-knowledge friend without our readers feeling we're talking down to them.

Need a bit of history? Have Oself dig for it, either searching the Internet or researching it in a library.

We can also, if we're skilled enough, tell it in conversation as Jack Finney does in the prologue of *From Time to Time*, where Bertrum O. Bush tells of watching a ship dock, but he tells it so we can see her tall stacks falling into line as she turns straight on, hear the whistle boom, watch the water boiling up around the tugs, and gaze at women's wide brimmed hats as big as umbrellas.

It's more work. It takes imagination. But aren't these our stock in trade?

Finally, we can get away with anything if we do it with skill and finesse. *Cold Mountain* by Charles Frazier is mostly all tell, and yet it was a well-received book. The same with *Snow Falling on Cedars* by David Guterson, which is not only mostly tell, but had a lot of flashbacks as well.

For the rest of us, I think the reader is better served by our dramatizing whatever we can. If we keep our story unfolding like real life before our readers' eyes, they will keep coming back for more.

The last thing one discovers in writing a book is what to put first.
—Blaise Pascal

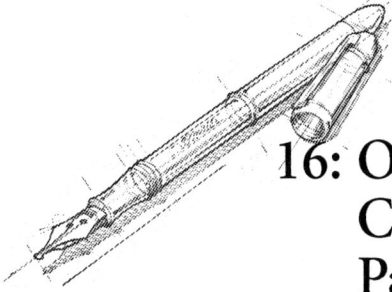

16: Opening Hooks—Come into My Parlor, Said the Spider

Pssst. Your Fly Is Open.

My friend, author Cyndy Mobley—*Code of Conflict*; *Rites of War*; *Rules of Command*—once mentioned this as an opening line for an agent query. It clarified for me what a query was supposed to be and I'll probably repeat it when we come to queries.

But it also works for opening hooks.

Pretend we are a book on a shelf in an airport—oh God, I can't believe I'm saying this—and a reader rushes in looking for something to distract him from takeoffs and landings and give him something to enjoy while he's suspended between the moon and New York City.

The cover is the first thing to catch the reader's eye. We have no control over that; usually it's strictly the publisher's call, but it doesn't hurt to make a suggestion. Anyway, the reader is attracted by our cover and picks us up. Maybe he ruffles though our pages like a deck of cards. If he sees margin to margin print all the way through, chances are his eyes glaze and he flops us back on the shelf.

But if he is encouraged by finding dialogue and shorter paragraphs—remember the use of white space?—then he'll turn to our front page. If we don't grab him now, snatch his eyeballs out of their sockets and hang on, he'll turn to another pretty cover. The fickle bastard.

> Reginald was tired, which was understandable, it being late in a rainy day, an overcast sky making it almost night. It had been a cold December. The freeze would probably last the month. He decided it was time to go home, even though it wasn't quitting time. He would take off early. Maybe if he was quick, he could beat the traffic, which slowed to a crawl when the streets slicked with rain. He would go home, have a drink, sink in an easy chair, watch the telly. Ah, if he had but known what was waiting for him he might have decided to spend the night in the office.

You are standing in the airport, five minutes to gate-time. Is that spiffy paragraph above gonna sell you?

Not likely.

Okay, I put a lot of slowdowns in it, like excessive clauses, but doesn't it have a plodding cadence, like lumbering behind a funeral cortege? Even the weak, archaic last line is only a pitiful attempt to generate suspense.

Compare:

"Pssst, your fly is open."

> Holy cow, he jerked sideways to the auditorium full of secretaries as he casually tried to zip up. Holy cow, it wouldn't budge. Ho-oo-ly cow, the damn thing was broken—
>
> "Pssst, your fly is open."
>
> "I heard, I heard." He snapped around to see two amused blue eyes staring back at him from the wings, a pretty smile reveling in his discomfort.

How about now? The first sentence pops the eyes open. The second paragraph throws us into frantic action and torques up the conflict. And the last sentence brings the embarrassment to a personal level and hints at a possible relationship, maybe sexual, maybe hostile, but definitely worth playing out.

There's another thing wrong with that first opening. Notice the little weather report? Do you say to yourself—oh boy, it's a cold December and the streets are wet, I can hardly wait to read this? And yet I see a lot of books start this way.

> It was a mild day in June, not too hot and not too cold, the humidity dry enough so the sweat didn't rise and still wet enough so the flowers didn't wilt.

Ho hum.

Weather adds a sense of place to the story, but it's background music, not the *1812 Overture*, not unless it's a major player in the story:

> Oself watched the killer roil down off the mountains. The wind and snow and sub-

> zero temperatures had already claimed twenty commuters. How many more would they find frozen in their homes?

Now that perked up our interest because the weather is a character in its own right, a killer stalking the landscape. We could also use it in a peripheral way to color an action.

> Oself turned from the rain-streaked window to study Sally's crossed legs. Long, shapely legs. Only one thing worth doing on a day like this. He gave her the full ivory grin that he practiced every morning in the mirror, and batted his baby blues.
>
> Yeah, momma.

Both of these paragraphs beg for our attention, the first because of the sense of danger and a waiting tragedy, the second because of a possible sexual encounter.

An opening hook, folks, is about advertising, not a letter to Aunt Mary. In days of yore, a writer could take three chapters to bring a reader into a novel. Today, because television and movies have introduced us into the world of instant gratification, we'd better do it in at least the first three pages, preferably in three paragraphs, even better, three sentences.

Look at magazine and newspaper ads for a clue to the kind of writing that has immediate impact. Of course, they usually have a picture to jerk us in, but the advertisers know they have only a second to grab us or it's over.

> Even Madam's most discriminating eye will find no flaw in the workmanship of

> our Ermine furs, cut in the latest styles, and ready to keep her warm on even the coldest nights at the opera.

This is a quote from a real nineteen-twenties advertisement for fur coats. Let's look at how it would be written today.

> Ermine. Rich. Luxurious. Wear it with diamonds and Gucci gowns. Or with nothing at all.

Get the idea? Look at the sentences—really only part sentences—blasting through like a series of chop punches, pow, pow, pow, and then slipping in that provocative little twist in the end. Do women get turned on at the thought of cavorting in only a fur coat? Maybe. But you can bet a man will be thinking about it when he buys it for his wife.

Another way to do it is to lull readers into thinking they know what you are going to say, then slip it to them.

> Beats there a heart so dead in the breast of man that it doesn't skip a beat to the sound of those resounding words—there once was a man from Nantucket.

Of course, I don't know where we'd go from there, but it gives us the idea. Once readers feel they know where the writer is going, they'll lose interest. So the idea is to lead them along a bit, then switch gears.

> Emily's hollow in the dunes opened up to an onshore breeze that flirted with red and yellow kites, sending

> them gamboling about the blue sky, and brought with it a taste of sea salt and a whiff of sunblock. The mumble of waves counterpointed an orchestration of shouts and squeals and whoops and laughter, while umbrellas and beach tents vied for sand-space with brown bodies lying on multicolored towels.
>
> But Emily's wide-open eyes didn't see it, wouldn't see it, not today, not tomorrow, not ever again.
>
> Sandpipers piped their short call as a flock ran along the beach, and a lone seagull flew overheard, giving out a plaintive cry.
>
> Emily's face swung toward the noise. Ever since her accident she had to see with her ears.

Okay, we have this nice carnival scene and just when we think everything is going to proceed serenely, bingo, we find out Emily is not seeing it, but it's phrased in such a way we are lulled into believing Emily had croaked. We have a murder here, but before that settles in, we find that's wrong as well. What we really have is a blind woman. Or do we?

Too many times we start our stories one chapter too soon. We go into a great exposition of the back-story or the setting. That can wait and be filled in later as we pace through the novel. We want to walk our readers into our story in the most provocative way. My personal preference is to jump in with an action, and if I can twist a sexual innuendo into it I'll try that hook as well. But the hook is part of our contract with our readers. We can't have a blast-action beginning to a literary story that is paced more slowly. But it doesn't have to be a drag either. Suppose we have a story based on a woman spending a winter alone at a lake with a lot of introspective stuff:

> The loon lay on a sun-bleached dock. The way its neck hung flaccidly over the side made it look obscene. Sally searched the shuttered houses that lined the mottled lake for signs of life. Nothing. Nor in the low, lead-gray sky. Only the wind, whistling through skeletal trees like a plaintive funeral dirge, broke the silence.
>
> But something had placed the loon there.
>
> Something to remember on cold nights.

Okay, okay, I talk a bit about the weather here, but it's used to show the isolation of the woman, which is part of the story. The dead loon should be symbolic of something as well.

The opening hook I used in my first published novel, *Bloody Bonsai*, was less dramatic than the sentence at the start of this chapter because it is a cozy mystery and I felt, right or wrong, it was slower paced than an action story. I centered it on the main character and tried to walk the reader into the story on the character's ambivalence:

> *You'll have a really good time*, they said.
> *You'll learn lotsa stuff*, they said.
> *You'll meet people*, they said.
> Yeah, right.

I mentioned the use of white space. Another thing I tried to do here was use the length of the sentences to draw the reader in. I leave it to you to judge its effectiveness.

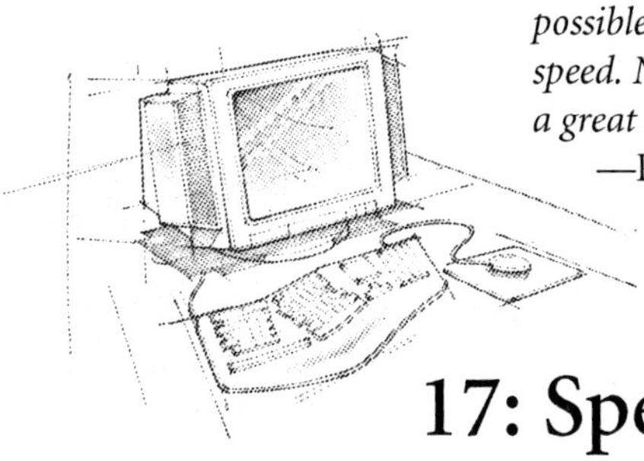

Always get to the dialogue as soon as possible. I always feel the thing to go for is speed. Nothing puts the reader off more than a great slab of prose at the start.
—P.G. Wodehouse

17: Speak to Me, Baby

Dialogue

What can I tell you about dialogue?

It has to ring true. It has to sound like real people speaking without it actually being a real conversation with all its um's and ah's and ya know's.

> "Good morning," Sally said.
> "Good morning," Sam replied.
> "And how are you this morning?" Sally interjected.
> "Just fine," Sam exclaimed. "And how are you?"

Snoooooze. Obviously we have to doctor our dialogue to render out the boring fat we all unconsciously slather on top of our own conversations.

> "Good morning," Sally said.
> "Hi," Sam said. "Have you seen the morning paper?"

We bypass the mundane and jump right into it, yet we must keep the ring of authenticity. Dialogue must also be part of our dramatizing. A sign of the rank amateur is to have two characters speak solely for the benefit of conveying information.

> "As you know, Sally, kumquats are our business. We are the biggest kumquat processors in the world."
>
> "Yes, as your secretary for five years, I know that. And I hear the kumquat crop has been devastated by drought this year, Sam."
>
> "Yes, Sally. We might have to layoff half our staff."
>
> "That will be a hardship on them, won't it, Sam, especially with Christmas two weeks away?"

Give me a break. Exposition is exposition, informing is informing, whether we have quotes around it or not. A dead giveaway is our old cliché, "as you know," for if Sally already knows, why is he telling her? Look also at how Sally and Sam keep using each other's name in their conversation. Does this sound natural? For a group of people, yes, but for two people in daily communication for five years? However, if the characters are trained professionals, such as a lawyer or a politician, then you might have them sprinkle each other's names about because it's one of the tricks they use to both aid themselves in remembering names and to ingratiate themselves by giving the impression they regard the other person as important.

So does this mean we can't convey information in dialogue? Yes we can, we just have to take the above example and dramatize it.

> Sally looked at the worry lines on Sam's face. "What's bothering you?"
>
> He shook his head and sighed, then nodded towards a big Christmas tree outside. "I have to lay off half my plant."
>
> "Now? At this time of year—"
>
> "Don't start." His jaw set. "You think I like it? We're reaping the benefit of last year's drought on the kumquat crop. I either lay them off or go into bankruptcy, then we all lose."

Well, it might not be perfect, but you get the idea.

If we want our dialogue to ring true, we have to pay attention to the conversation of real people we are trying to characterize. Copy it down if you can. Keep notes. Remember our journal? And pay attention to people speaking in malls, metros and movie houses. My wife raises her eyes whenever she catches me eavesdropping on another's conversation, and I'm always doing it. But if I did it in a group of writers, if we can ever stop each other from speaking, it might be taken as a sign of our craft.

Always picture the people speaking, then eliminate everything but the essentials, those things that advance the story, add to characterization, or give a sense of place. Dialogue in a fast, easy read will make up 40- to 60-percent of our story, so we have to get it right.

Speaker Attributes

Look back to that terrible example where Sally and Sam kept using each other's name. Notice the speaker attributes—she said, he replied, she interjected, and he exclaimed—these are also the mark of a rank amateur, although Robert Ludlum does this stuff all the time...one of the reasons I don't read Robert Ludlum.

At first blush this might seem the way to go, especially if we read our work aloud. I listen to audio books a lot, and Ed McBain a lot. His writing bothers my wife because of all the he-said's, she-said's that might continue for twenty lines—well, actually it's Haws said, Carilla said, Myer said. But McBain, who also writes under the name Evan Hunter, writes to be read, and for print he is right on.

Speaker attributes of he-said, she-said disappear for readers as part of the quotation marks surrounding the dialogue. Just as our minds are trained to hear dialogue when we come to quotation marks, rather than say quote and unquote to ourselves, so they are trained not to hear "who said," but only attribute the conversation to a speaker. But if you throw in a whole lot of he exclaimed's and she interjected's, they'll stand out like a squashed frog on a white wall. What's even worse is he/she lied. Suppose in narration Oself breaks a dish and later his mother asked who did it. "Not me," he lied. Duh. Are we so dumb we have to be told he lied? Don't restate the obvious.

Use *he said, she said* all the time. Even reversing the order—said he—calls attention to the attribute, although I find myself doing it occasionally. Hey, I'm human.

Of course, if our dialogue is a question, he/she asked should be substituted for he/she said. I sometimes try to pose a rhetorical question using said, like—"Waddya say?" he said—but my editor always changes it to ask, and, wanting to be published, I acquiesce. She insists, as well, I change "till" to "until" although my dictionary says both are valid and mean the same thing. We have agreed that I will use "until" *till* I have a best seller.

We also want to use attributes without adverb modifiers. Sometimes this becomes so obvious it starts a fad, as with the short-lived Tom Swifties mania from the seventies, named after the early 20th century book series of the same name:

> "I'm dying of thirst," Tom said dryly.
>
> "We could freeze to death in this blizzard," Tom said coldly.

But the same can be said of using an adverb for an emotion:

> "Now, Dear, we shouldn't be doing that," Sally said angrily.

> "I want to go to bed with you," Sally said shyly.

If the dialogue doesn't carry the emotion, a modifier won't cut it. If the dialogue does carry the emotion, the adverb is unnecessary and detracting, actually weakening the verb instead of strengthening it:

> "Cut that out," Sally said.

> "I was wondering—oh, how do I say this—maybe, um, sometime maybe we should think about going to bed together," Sally said.

But there are some exceptions to using modifiers, like when there is no other way to describe the manner of speech:

> "Keep in the shadows," Oself said softly (quietly, lowly).
>
> "Keep in the shadows," Oself whispered.

Some writers disparage "whispered," and it does break our he-said, she-said advice, but I use it because the one word conveys speaker volume. I might also use "murmured" for the same reason. Does that mean it's okay? I think any of the above examples work so long as they aren't overused. In a short scene, once is enough to set it up, and maybe a reminder for longer tracts. We also might tell how it sounds if it's important or character dependent, but even here we still use "said."

> "Hi, I'm Senator Rafferty," he said, using the full imperial power of his sonorous voice.

We could have broken that dialogue to bring the speaker attribute on more quickly had we desired.

> "Hi," the old man said with the full imperial power of his sonorous voice, "I'm Senator Rafferty."

But speaker attributes must always be at the break of a sentence, or at the break of a clause where a comma would normally occur.

> "Hi, I'm Senator," he said, using the full imperial power of his sonorous voice, "Rafferty."

In an extreme case like this we can see it right off, but less obvious ones won't work either.

> "I saw them heading down," Oself
> said, "the trail towards town."

More subtle ones may get by, but it won't feel right to the reader, perhaps without knowing why. I've read some books where the writer does this stuff all the time, but it doesn't make for easy reading.

At the same time, dialogue does not always have to be correct English.

> "Don't wanna do that. Any a youse
> guys wanna do that?"

What's important is that it rings true in the reader's mind for the character saying it.

Which brings us to exclamation points.

> "Would you please get out of the
> house and go outside, dear!"

If the words don't carry it, the exclamation point is not going to help.

> "Go. Now. Outside."

And if the words do carry it, the exclamation point is not necessary. Where it might be needed is in a one-word command.

> "Out!"

But in the course of a novel we should be able to count them on one hand.

Tags, Beats, Body Language

Tags, beats, and body language are also used as dialogue identifiers, especially in writing group scenes.

Tags are particular words, actions, or mannerism that have been previously built into a single character. We mentioned in character profiles that if Oself blinks nervously all the time, we can use the identifying tag when he reenters a scene:

> Oself came into the room, big eyes blinking away.

In dialogue we can use the tag in place of a speaker attribute.

> "Why do that?" Blink, blink. "It's unnecessary."

Tags can also be manners of speech, so long as they are character specific.

> Jim Dandy raised his eyes to the heavens and held out his hands. "Great. Just great."

This is one of the things grouchy old Jim Dandy says in the Elderhostel mysteries, and he uses it early in every book, grousing around because things are not going just the way he planned. For a reader who has been following the series, this is like a touchstone, immediately reacquainting them to the character, and hopefully bringing a smile. For a new reader it sets up the tag. After I use this a few times connected to the name, readers will tag this to Jim Dandy, so that when they see, "Great, just great," they'll attribute it to him even without an identifier.

But the tag has to be character specific. We couldn't use "Good morning," as a tag, because everyone says that.

Beats are small bits of action specific to a scene. If conversation takes place while repairing a car, it's logical to intersperse the dialogue with an action, which we can use as a beat to identify the speaker:

> "This is necessary." Oself tightened the nuts on the engine block. "The car will never get there unless it's fixed."

We can also use body language as an identifier, a better indication of a character's true feelings than what he/she says. We can use it to reinforce or contradict the dialogue:

> "Who wants to go for ice cream?" Oself asked.
>
> Jane stared sideways at him, her arms and legs crossed, hands clenched into fist-balls. "I'd love to go with you."
>
> Sally's eyebrows arched. "I'd love to go, too." She leaned forward on her chair as if ready to spring to her feet.

Sally is obviously excited about going with Oself, but Jane, contradicting her dialog, probably wants nothing to do with it.

We can do a lot with body language, many times even using it to replace dialogue. He shook his head. She nodded. Also think of the other facial expressions and body actions that can reveal what a character is thinking. He can shrug, cross his arms, raise his eyebrows, lean against a wall, rub his chin. At the same time we can make them into a beat or identifier by adding a name. And if the specific action is singular for that character, it becomes a tag like the "blink, blink" we used above.

> "I don't know." Oself rubbed beside his nose twice, then finished the motion by tracing his finger across his lips in that peculiar action of his. "Tell you what." He pointed the finger toward the door. "Let's see how the ballistics match."

From the body language it should be obvious that Oself has paused in his dialogue to think. If Oself has used these particular actions a couple of times before, we can eliminate "in that peculiar action of his," and substitute "he" for "Oself," because this will then have become a tag. Now you might argue this spends more words than "John thought a moment," but that is *telling* us while the body language *shows* us, giving us a picture as a real world action.

No conversation takes place in a vacuum. People normally don't freeze and use only their mouths when they speak. By using beats, tags, and body language we keep our readers grounded in what's going on around them, advance the narration, define our characters, and maintain interest by operating on more than one level.

Subject Shift in Dialogue

The thing about shifting subjects in dialogue is that we have to make it seem natural. We hinted at it in our last example.

> "Yes," Sally said, "it is a nice day.
> Look at those big fluffy clouds in the sky.
> Did you study the constitution?"

Say what? The transition to that last sentence is too abrupt. Does it happen in real conversation? Yes. But this is not real conversation. If we had set up the character to speak this way normally, or if the narration revealed school work had been uppermost on the speaker's mind, it would work, but then it should elicit a response.

> "Yes," Sally said, "it is a nice day.
> Look at those big fluffy clouds in the sky.
> Did you study the constitution?"
> "Wow, where did that come from?"

A better way is to use body language to prepare the reader for a subject shift in Sally's thinking.

> "Yes," Sally said, "it is a nice day.
> Look at those big fluffy clouds in the sky."
> Sally turned to Oself. "Did you study the constitution?"

Or better yet:

> "Yes," Sally said, "it is a nice day.
> Look at those big fluffy clouds in the sky."

> She glanced down to the school book in her lap. "Did you study the constitution?"

The second example leads the reader right into the reason for the change of subject so that we may not need a setup in narrative, especially if the reader knows about the school work from past reading. Any action break will give us a natural place to shift subjects.

> "Yes," Sally said, "it is a nice day. Look at those big fluffy clouds in the sky."
>
> They walked on a bit.
>
> "Did you study the constitution?" Sally asked.

If we were rewriting all this for a final draft, we would drop the cliché "fluffy" and eliminate "in the sky" because, duh, where else are we going to find clouds? Was that a gotcha?

We can also have an abrupt subject shift in the POV character.

> Oself couldn't get the picture of Sally holding John's hand out of his mind. Was she having an affair?
>
> "Oh, look," Sally said, "isn't that a beautiful sky?"
>
> "Yes, look at all the fluffy—Why were you talking to John?"

Sally might not be ready for Oself's shift, but the reader is. Shifting thought and subjects is not a big thing; almost any pause will do, but a piece of body language can help lead the reader into the transition.

> "Yes," Sally said, "it is a nice day. Look at those big clouds." Sally took Oself's hand in hers. "It's really been a great vacation, hasn't it?"

> "Yes," Sally said, "it is a nice day. Look at those big clouds." Sally raised her eyebrows, turned down her lips, and shook her head. "Too bad our vacation is over tomorrow."

> "Yes," Sally said, "it is a nice day. Look at those big clouds." Sally put her hand to her chin rubbing it. "Heading back tomorrow. Have to remember to pick up our mail."

Finally, an ambiguous conversational response such as, "Um," or "Uh huh," could indicate casual agreement, but could also indicate inattention, meaning the character is thinking of something else, and so our readers would be ready if we followed it with a change of subject.

> "Oh," Sally said, "what a nice day. Look at those big clouds."
>
> "Uh huh. Do you know where I put the car keys?"

So far we've only handled conversation between two or three people. But what happens if our protagonist sits down for dinner with a group of people?

Go on to the next chapter and find out.

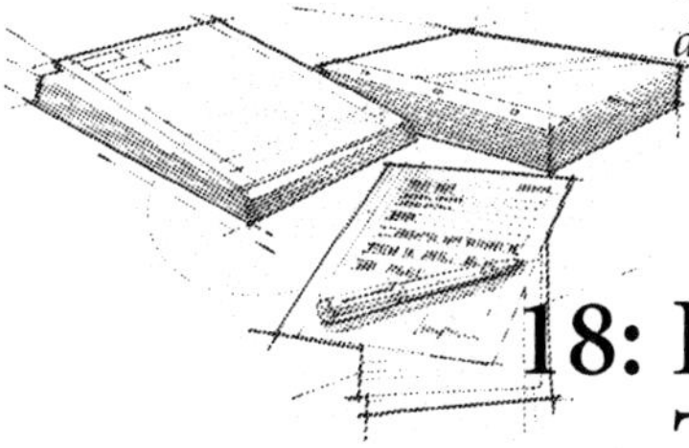

Sometimes you need to write garbage just to keep going, not knowing what you need and don't.

18: Look Who's Talking

Dialogue in Group Scenes

I often find writers avoiding group scenes because they're afraid of writing dialogue for more than two characters. But it's like anything else, folks, you write it badly and then rework it till it's right. In writing the Elderhostel Mystery series, I'm always having to write scenes involving people having a meal together, so it's gotten easier for me; not easy, easier.

We can ease the burden through the use of: speaker attributes, he-said/she-said; beats, bits of action specific to the scene; tags, mannerisms particular to a character; and body language. Let's number these lines to facilitate breaking it down.

Jim piled food on his plate and carried it to the table.

1. "Hello, Jim." The black-haired Sana greeted him in her sing-song India English. "We were indeed wondering if you would make it to tea."

2. "Made a quick trip into Bolder Harbor," he said, spreading lunch booty around his place setting. "Needed a sprayer."

3. "'Tis easy to see you believe in a hardy lunch."

4. "A good lunch sets you right up for a good dinner." Smiles around the table and giggling from Tiffany Crew. "When I get home I'll do extra exercises for a couple of days to take it off."

5. "How about a week?" Dodee said.

6. "How about a month?" Kelly Massey added.

7. The female half of the Miettlinens gave a pursed lipped smile, the first signs of humor. "How about a year?"

8. Clarence Harmoney forked in some potatoes and gravy, and turned to Simon Crew, "I'm in garbage. That is, I own a garbage company. So, you retired?"

9. "Semi-retired. I'm a stockbroker. No clients anymore, but I'm always working on my own portfolio."

10. "Uh huh. That how you met your wife, she a client of yours?"

11. Jim put down his fork. Clarence had asked the question they all entertained; if the twenty-something roommate was his wife.

12. Tiffany dabbed a napkin to her lips. "Not hardly."

13. "Actually"—Simon adjusted his hexagonal glasses and patted her hand—"I was a client of hers."

Okay, let's break it down.

Paragraph 1: We identify Sana through a tag—her peculiar English—and by her greeting she is obviously talking to Jim who has just walked up to the table.

Paragraph 2: We use a speaker attribute, but don't need to identify Jim by name because, even in a group, he is responding to Sana, but the beat of spreading lunch booty clinches it.

Paragraph 3 & 4: We don't need identifiers here because the reader will assume this is the continuing dialogue of Jim and Sana responding to one another.

Paragraph 5 & 6: Dodee and Kelly chime in here with speaker attributes.

Paragraph 7: Now a beat introduces Mrs. Miettlinens.

Paragraph 8: We change speakers again with a beat—Clarence shoveling food in his face—and use a bit of body language, turning to Simon Crew, to shift the dialogue.

Paragraph 9: We don't need an identifier here because Clarence directed his question to Simon. The reader will assume it is his answer unless there's an indication to the contrary.

Paragraph 10: No identifier here either because, like 3 & 4, readers will assume the two are responding to one another as long as the conversation continues without interruption.

Paragraph 11: Jim has some business here, reiterating what has been said privately in previous chapters and giving it emphasis.

Paragraph 12: Tiffany pops in with a beat.

Paragraph 13: And finally, we have a tag—Simon adjusting his hexagonal glasses—as an identifier. Had we fully developed this tag, we wouldn't even have needed to use Simon's name.

We could have carried this same thing off with nothing but speaker attributes, as we mentioned Ed McBain does in his books with he-said/she-said. We could also have done it only with beats, or only tags, or only body language, but I think this would have been strained and dicey. Using all of these tools allows us to give it variety, to emphasize certain things, add to our characterization, advance the narration, and to keep the interest in what's going on as the conversation takes place. Unbroken conversations, like unbroken narration, can get bor-ring.

One last thing about dialogue between more than two people. When a conversation is bouncing back and forth between two people and a third suddenly speaks up, especially if it is a long or a complicated sentence that can't be broken, the speaker attribute, beat, or tag should begin the sentence. This immediately lets the reader know who's speaking rather than hearing the dialogue and then figuring out who it belongs to.

> Oself said, "Sorry to cut in, but I think you're both wrong."

An alternative to this, if the sentence can be quickly broken, is to put the identifier at the first break.

> "Sorry to cut in," Oself said, "but I think you're both wrong."

If it is a short sentence, I think the reader will take it in all at one time.

> "No way," Oself said.

Dialogue Under Stress

Stress alters our speech. When we are sitting around over coffee our sentences are rambling, full of redundancy and ahs and ohs and ums.

> Oself sat on the porch swing and gazed down at the Sheriff's four-year-old boy trying to pick up the gun from the bench where the sheriff had placed it.
>
> "Well, I swear, he sure is a determined cuss, ain't he. That thing, from handle to tip, has got to be bigger than he is. You damn sure it ain't loaded?"
>
> "Um, not only not loaded, but, ah, I put the safety on, did it myself, because, you know, you can't be too careful, ah, with guns and young critters."

But put the character under stress and the long rambling dialogue gives way to short outbursts. The more stress we apply, the shorter the sentences, finally giving way to monosyllable words.

> The boy picked up the gun in two hands and pointed toward the porch.

> Oself glanced at the sheriff and back to the boy. "Sure that damn thing's unloaded?"
>
> "I told you, I'm sure it's not—"
>
> A shot rang out and a bullet slapped into the porch post.
>
> "Sonofabitch." Oself jumped to his feet. "It's loaded, it's loaded."
>
> "Put it down. Johnny, put it down."
>
> Another shot rang out, splintering the porch swing.
>
> "Loaded. Loaded."
>
> "Down. Put down. Now."

So the more stress, fear or anger we apply, the shorter our dialogue becomes.

The other thing about stress is that no matter how hard a person might try to hide his speech or speech pattern of origin, in times of stress he will always revert to his home language and sentence structure.

If a woman grows up with Cockney English but is trained to speak the language of the upper class, in times of stress she will slip back into Cockney. There is that great racetrack scene in *My Fair Lady* where Eliza Doolittle, speaking impeccably up to the point where her horse is racing for the finish line, suddenly bursts out, "C'mon, move ya bloomin' arse."

This will hold true be it for a native dialect, a foreign language, or even the type of expletives a person might use. The outbursts of a genteel woman at the turn of the twentieth century will be far different from one at the turn of the twenty-first century, where "You dirty dog," turns to "You shit," and perhaps stronger.

Which brings up the use of words we might not use in polite language. For instance, the word "fuck" has lost its ability to shock. When I was a teenager, being of an older generation, if a woman used that word I would have been stunned, although we boys used it freely among ourselves. And if I said it in front of my mother, I would have landed in the middle of next week, which is another colloquialism from those days.

But if you visit any college campus today you will hear men and women using "fuck" as casually as "the cat's pajamas" of a hundred years ago. So if we want it to shock our readers, we need to use it sparingly, maybe only in times of extreme stress, as at the climactic scene at the novel's end.

On the other hand, if we are building a young character in today's world, he/she could well use that word in every other sentence. The problem here arises in our readership. Some older women are so offended by the word they will not read a book where it is liberally sprinkled about.

I had a letter from a fan who said she loved my book, *Bloody Bonsai*, up until page two hundred plus where Jim Dandy used "that word." She didn't like the word and she knew Jim Dandy would not use it, which was a surprise to me considering I created him. But readers are like that.

What is strange is that the aversion is only to "fuck," while almost any other cuss word will get by. So, we have to decide who our readership is, who we are willing to—forgive me—write off, and at the same time be true to what we are trying to portray. And if we can use a substitute.

Dialect

Speaking in a dialect is part of our heritage in this polyglot country of immigrants, as well as speaking in colloquialisms and slang. We have it much easier than in England where we also would have to worry about class. In using dialect we try to give the impression of a regional variation or foreign language using standard English. The trouble with using dialect is it has to sound right without using fractured words.

> "Why do dat gu' tret me that'a way," he said.

This won't cut it. At one time it might have, if you look back to the early nineteen hundreds, but today's reader won't spend the time trying decipher it.

> "Hello, Jim," the black-haired Sana greeted in her sing-song India English, "We were indeed wondering if you would make it to tea."
>
> "Made a quick trip into Bolder Harbor," he said, spreading lunch booty around his place setting. "Needed a sprayer."
>
> "'Tis easy to see you believe in a hearty lunch."

These lines, repeated from our dinner table above, identify Sana's speech as India English here, so the "sing-song" sound will add lilt to the subsequent sentence. We depend on the reader to do that. We also use words that give flavor to India English like "'tis," "hearty," "indeed," and "tea" for dinner. If we want to use dialect we need simulate it through word use and altered sentence structure.

> "I should charge both a ya, but—you're leaving Friday?" Jim nodded. Belinda Smith nodded in return. "I figure Sonny put you through enough stuff already. Go on." But then the woman detective stopped them as they reached the door. "Hey," the dark eyes glaring from her chocolate face. "I'm going back home to bed. Don't wanna hear about you guys again. Don't wanna be woken up anymore and drug out in the middle of the night. Knowhatamean?"

This character is a woman detective in New Jersey. The "Don't wanna," sounded right, without the preceding "I." Also the "Knowhatamean" sounded right, although a few people thought it was over the top.

> "May I help you, suh?" she asked, her voice dancing with the lilting inflection of the West Indies.
>
> "I'm here for the Elderhostel," Jim said. "Is there still space for me to park my car?"
>
> "Yes suh, what you must do, because this next street is one direction, go up to the second corna, take three rights and come back to the side of the hotel. If you will then honk your horn I shall raise the gate for you. When you come back I shall assign you a room."

Okay, I did use two altered words here, "suh" and "around the 'corna,'" but I don't think anyone will have trouble knowing and hearing them. A few fractured words, whose meaning is obvious, sprinkled sparingly about will not slow the read, and they help with the inflection in a long conversation. But we do have to trust the readers to make the connection when we tell them her voice danced with a West Indian lilt, and to apply it to the woman's conversation. We help them hear that by using a sentence structure and idiom to reflect it, "Yes suh, what you must do, because this next street is one direction, go up to the second corna…"

> "So!" The word spit out of the darkness and hovered in the general direction of the SS Death's Head cap. "What did you find in the attic?"
>
> Jon recognized the timbre of voice, but couldn't bring the tone into focus, as if a soprano was singing bass.
>
> "Come, come, *Herr* General." The shadow in the black uniform was moving towards the door. "Have you suddenly got laryngitis? It is a simple question, yes? What was so interesting in the attic, hum? So interesting you kept me waiting?"
>
> Did the guy have a gun?
>
> "So," the black figure at the door now, "should I shoot you, *mein* General, hum?"
>
> Oh, hell, he did have a gun.
>
> "Or should I give you the spanking you deserve?"

Here we altered our sentence structure and sprinkled in a few foreign words to simulate characters talking in German. We don't actually say they are speaking in German, but can you not hear it? Foreign words, again, should be italicized, which is always indicated in a manuscript by underlining.

So, *achtung*, you vill get dialogue right und you vill have a good time doing it, or else.

Character-Specific Dialogue

We've already talked about this a bit when we talked about tags, words a character uses often, but now we're talking about the grammar he uses in general conversation.

> "Ain't gonna do that. Any a youse guys gonna do that?"

The way our characters speak is an indication of the background we have given them. This dialogue probably indicates someone from New York City. I might have overdone it for this example, but I don't know of any other area that would use "youse guys." We could change the location by changing three words.

> "Ain't gonna do that. Any *of you all* gonna do that?"

Now we probably have someone from the south. We could clinch if with "y'all," but that's gotten to be a bit of a cliché. And we could change the education level by changing a couple of words.

> "*Don't wanna* do that. Any of you all *wanna* do that?"

And sophistication level by changing two words and adding a few.

> "*I surely* don't *want to* do that. Any of you all *want to* do that?"

From this we can realize the importance of choosing each word of dialogue to reflect our character.

> "You'll forgive me if I seem paranoid, Cranfield. Someone burgled my house and I have deemed it necessary to obtain security," Buckeys said, nodding toward the burley, crewcut man across the table. "It does tend to make one suspicious. Allow me to introduce you to my philatelist acquaintance, Harry Zollern," he said, indicating the owlish man. A waiter approached; Buckeys waved him away. "If you would allow Zollern to examine the merchandise we can conclude our transaction before we order lunch."

Obviously we couldn't mix the first example of "youse guys" with this one and retain credibility, unless the second character, Buckeys, used it as a joke or an offbeat point of emphasis. This character is not only far better educated, but just from this little bit of dialogue we can deduce he's miles above him in the economic strata, indicated by the bodyguard and the off handed dismissal of the waiter. There are also the more subtle signs that indicate Buckeys position in life such as: not introducing his bodyguard; introducing Harry Zollern to Cranfield, but not the other way around; and in using both their last names without a "Mr." to signal they are just the help.

But suppose all this was just an act?

It would show up in times of stress.

Place any of us in extreme danger, a gun to the head, a car hurtling toward us, and we will revert to our base language, be it German, French, lowdown New Orleans slang.

An example of this is the last words on most flight recorders before a plane plunges into the side of a mountain. "Oh, shit."

Just like we will revert to our base language, so to will our language reflect that of our parents and siblings.

My twin sons always say, "Deserves him right," instead of "Serves him right." They are the only ones of my five sons who use that, but being twins they reinforce one another. However, all my sons say "old timey," like "old timey cars," and I hear it in my grandchildren.

If a father often says, "What am I, a Rockefeller?" chances are you will hear some form of that in the children—"You think I'm a Rockefeller?"—and perhaps in his nephews and nieces as well. So if we are building characters from the same family, using the same phrases among them would reinforce that authenticity, even if only subliminally, for our readers.

Just like similar phrases are used within a family, so are they used in certain areas. "So what do you think, hey," the "hey" being attributed to Canadians, and "That's just precious, darlin'," is typical of a woman of the south.

We should be listening for these things to set our characters apart.

Tracking a Character's Dialogue

Say we get our characters to start out talking in an individual manner, is that enough?

We also need them to be consistent.

We can't have a woman saying "That's just precious, darlin'," in one place and "Youse guys ain't worth a shit, man," somewhere else. Admittedly, that's extreme, and we may get away with more subtle changes, but we'll reinforce the character with consistency.

So how do we do that?

Remember how we talked about breaking out all our POV characters and reading them sequentially, as if they were a book unto themselves? We need to do the same for dialogue.

Aw, c'mon, that's a lot of work.

Easy reading is damn hard writing.

If we want to make our dialogue the best we can make it, we'll pull out all the places where a particular character is speaking and read through them, making changes for consistency.

There are no shortcuts to good writing.

My friend and teacher, Marcie Heidish, told me the ideal dialogue is such that we should be able to tell who is speaking without any identifiers, just from the way they string their words together.

I don't think I'm there yet, but I'm working on it.

Nothing can happen nowhere. The locale *of the happening always colours the happening, and often, to a degree, shapes it. Plot having pre-decided what is to happen, scene, scenes, must be so found, so chosen, as to give happening the desired force. Almost anything drawn from "real life"—house, town, room, park, landscape—will almost certainly be found to require some distortion for the purpose of plot.*
—Elizabeth Bowen

19: Where Are We?

Sense of Place

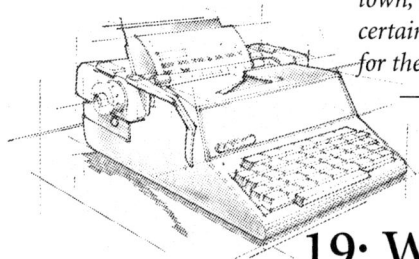

Place is background. It's the set and props behind stage actors. It's the backdrop of people passing by in a movie.

Only, in fiction, it's much more.

It's what gives our readers the feeling of walking along narrow stone streets in Jerusalem; climbing creaky stairs of a gloomy old house in Transylvania; listening to the whisper of shifting desert sands that's gritting up our ears and eyes.

The problem is in knowing how much is enough. In the old cowpoke books, Zane Gray could get away with taking three pages to describe a sunset. Try that now and our writing will never see—forgive me—the light of day.

Most of us think of Place as just a few lines to tell us what the walls look like, and if we're just zipping through something on a train, that might be enough. But we should regard each Place description as providing us with four opportunities. The first, of course, is to put our readers in the scene, the second is to include props and information that will be needed in the story, third is to reflect our characters, and fourth, to set the mood for what is happening.

> A tang of sea salt rode on the chill of the early spring air. Militant waves, streaked with beer foam, marched in from a leaden eternity. They rose up like phalanxes against the New Jersey shore, and with a roaring charge came smashing and crumbling and bumbling and bouncing onto the sand, deserted of even the bravest of beachcombers.

A lot of things happening here. Once again we use the senses to trigger memory responses from our readers: the taste and smell of sea salt; the sound of the roaring charge; the feel of the chill of the air; and the sight of beer foam streaks on the militant waves as they crash against the shore. There's also a lot of action here. Long static descriptions will stop our story. Notice the "smashing and crumbling and bumbling and bouncing," words decreasing in violence to trigger the impression of wave action as it breaks and moves up the sand, and ends with "deserted of even the bravest of beachcombers" to not only give the feeling of loneliness and isolation, but the impression of the wave sliding back into the sea.

We also try to trigger a dark and foreboding mood by use of heavy words: militant; phalanxes; leaden eternity; and deserted; and by increasing the violence as we pace through the scene: march in; rise up; a roaring charge; and the attack on the beach. Rather than using the old cliché, "if I only knew then what I know now," we place our readers in the scene and trust them to come up with the right conclusion.

Does it all work?

Perhaps not, and maybe only on a subconscious level, but if we were actually at that beach, would we be consciously aware of everything, or would we be reacting on all levels to things going on around us? That's what we're trying to do when we work to create Place.

Let's change the mood by looking at a description we've used before:

> An onshore breeze flirted with red and yellow kites gamboling about the blue sky, and brought with it a taste of sea salt and a whiff of sunblock. The rumble of waves against the New Jersey shore counterpointed an orchestration of shouts and squeals and whoops and laughter, while umbrellas and beach tents vied for sand-space with brown bodies lying on multicolored towels.

Same beach, huh? What's the feel now? Lighthearted. Carnival. Vacation time. We create the mood by using bright colors: red and yellow kites; multicolored towels; sunblock. We use words to trigger playfulness: flirting; kites; gamboling; squeals; whoops; laughter. We deliberately use sunblock, rather than a tanning lotion or a brand name, because it operates on more than one level, for protection against the sun, but also implying a sun strong enough to protect against.

Once again we bring in the senses to aid in triggering memory responses, and we dramatize rather than inform. If we had said, "the kids were making a lot of noise," we would have informed, but not engaged. Instead we used the rumble of waves counterpointed by "shouts and squeals and whoops and laughter," to trigger in our readers the memory of lying on one of those multicolored beach towels, with their eyes closed, and hearing the cacophony of sound that plays as background.

Two more things about both these descriptions.

They are short, squeezing each word to operate on more than one level, and use action to keep them flowing. It takes far more words to explain them than to use them.

They also impart information needed for the story.

We could have started out by saying, "It was a cold, spring day on the New Jersey shore." It gives us the environs of our story, which we need, but it's just informing us. It's like saying, "Look, folks, this is where our story is."

So, instead, we place our readers right there on the New Jersey shore, let them feel the cold of the dreary spring day, or the warmth of the bright summer day, and they know where they are because it's all around them.

Getting tired of sand in your shoes and salt on your sunshades?

> The third key on Oself's key ring fit the lock. He slipped it and stole inside into a pale-yellow hallway. He stood with his back against the door, engulfed by the house's warmth, and breathed in a cozy hint of furniture wax, a flowery room freshener, and perhaps a taste of home-cooked meals. He craned his neck and peered up an exposed staircase on his left, where he heard the soft ticktock of a far-off clock, his pounding heart triple-timing its dogged rhythm.
>
> A living room opened onto his right. He cat-pawed halfway through it

and peeked left into a formal dining room. Empty. He scooted around a polished table for twelve and eased into the buff of a stainless steel kitchen at the rear, cut left into a paneled library with leather furniture, then circled back up the hall. He paused at the stairwell, hand on banister, and glanced from picture frame to picture frame of matted postage stamps stair-stepped along the wall up to the second floor.

There was still time to get out.

"Hello? Anybody home?"

Only the distant ticktock answered him.

Okay, folks, so what's happening here?

First of all, notice again an attempt to play on the senses, the hint of furniture wax and home-cooked meals to give us smell and taste, the ticktock of the clock, the house's warmth, and all the visuals to help Place our readers in the scene. There's also his pounding heart to give us the feeling of tension; someone apparently breaking in and cat-pawing through the house to see if he is alone.

But what else does it tell us?

It's an upscale house, right? Twelve-person table, formal dining room, stainless steel kitchen, paneled library with leather furniture. Which also tells us something about those who live there, people well educated and in the upper economic strata. But doesn't it also give us the layout of the house? Without laboring our reader with the living room in the front, kitchen in the back, stairs on the side, we show it to them as the guy runs around. Also notice the framed stamps on the wall. They add to the ambiance, but they could also be props for later use. We need all this information to follow the story, but rather than stop everything with a static explanation, we slip it into the action of the character.

Let's carry this a bit further with a description we used in an earlier chapter.

> "Hello? Anybody home?"
>
> Only the distant ticktock answered him.
>
> Oself scanned the living room: big stuffed chairs and settee with a flowery pattern; framed oils on dappled green walls, none he recognized, but he liked their technique; a marble fireplace with a portrait above, maybe 19th century; mauve carpet; and hanging out on a cocktail table with some silver-framed photographs was a remote control.
>
> But he could see no television. He picked it up and pressed the button.
>
> A gas-log fire poofed on in the fireplace.
>
> Your momma!

Okay, I used an exclamation point, but notice it's short and I need to give it force. It's the character's reaction to the fireplace poofing on, and, okay, there's no such word, but doesn't it give us the picture?

We've said the house tells us something about the people who live there, and at the same time we are giving our readers a picture of the living room, but aren't we also giving them clues to Oself's character? Look at the things he notices. Pale yellow hallway and framed postage stamps from the first section; in the second, framed oils on dappled green walls, mauve carpet, and a portrait above the marble fireplace. There's also the fact that while he doesn't recognize the oils, he likes their technique, and he guesses the portrait is probably 19th century.

So what does that tell us?

Certainly he is someone interested in color. He apparently knows enough about art and artists to make a judgment of technique: not recognizing the painters implies he would recognize a bunch, and he has to know art history to postulate the portrait's date. Taking these things into account, we have set the reader up for Oself to be an interior decorator, someone in the arts, a gallery owner, a teacher, or an artist.

If we left out the paintings and portrait we would still see the room, but would we have the same character?

> Oself cat-pawed straight through the living room, paused at the dining room with place settings for a formal dinner of twelve, paused again in a spotless stainless steel kitchen, then cut left to a paneled library and circled back up the hall. He hesitated at the foot of the stairs, hand on the banister, some old copies of Bon Appetite waiting on the second step for someone to carry them up.
>
> There was still time to get out.
>
> "Hello? Anybody home?"
>
> Only the distant ticktock answered him.
>
> He passed through the living room again, stopped in the dining room, gazed at the china place settings and polished

> English silverware, and exchanged the cocktail forks for the salad forks. He sauntered into the kitchen and breathed in a rich aroma of spices, herbs, a hint of past culinary extravagances. Henckels knives stuck out of a butcher-block holder. All-Clad pots hung from a rack about the stove.
>
> He opened the double doors of the refrigerator.
>
> Your momma!

What's Oself now?

Obviously his attention is on the kitchen and what's in the refrigerator. At first blush we might think of him as a chowhound, but that wouldn't account for him switching the silverware. That takes a special knowledge, the same with noticing what kind of knives and pots are in the kitchen. So we're left with a possible gourmet, caterer, butler, or a chef.

But if Oself is in the arts in the first example, or in the culinary arts in the second, what the hell is he doing in the house?

> Bernie slipped the lock, sneaked inside, and shut the door behind. Only a far off ticktock disturbed the silence. He set his duffel on the floor and checked behind the door and in a hall closet for an alarm, then craned his neck and gazed up the staircase, down the long hall, and turned to the living room.
>
> Pictures hung on the wall in gilt frames. He pursed his lips and nodded. He cat-pawed straight through to the

dining room and paused to look at the silverware, shrugged, and continued on through the stainless steel kitchen to a library in the rear corner of the house. Books lined the walls, each with a like-new jacket protected by a clear plastic cover. First editions? He raised his eyebrows and blew air out through puffed lips, then circled back up the hall. He hesitated at the foot of the stairs, hand on the banister, studied framed postage stamps hanging on the wall and shrugged again.

He cracked the front door, peeked out, and turned to gaze up the stairs again.

"Hello? Anybody home?"

Only the distant ticktock answered him.

Bernie smiled and shut the front door. He picked up his duffel and moved into the living room. An inlaid humidor sat prominently on a side cabinet. A gold lighter and cigar clipper rested beside it. He took out one of the cigars, smelled it, clipped off the end, dropping the clipper in his duffel, and lit the cigar. He took a deep draw and blew the smoke through "O" shaped lips. He dropped the lighter in his duffel, and added the humidor as well.

He glanced over the paintings again and sauntered over to the one

> above the fireplace, studied the sides of the frame, then swung it open like a door to reveal a small wall safe.
>
> Your mamma!

Okay, we might not have known what Oself was doing in the house, either Oself, but we sure know why Bernie is there.

Once again, notice there's action involved in all of these examples. We don't stop the story to present a static scene.

> "Bring bug spray?" Jim said.
>
> He glanced at his passenger, but Dodee Swisher kept her head full of soft curls, about the color of ripened wheat, buried in the information sheet on her lap. She wore a light-blue jean shirt with red plaid showing at the collar and cuffs, cream colored denim pants, and soft loafers on her feet, her trim body a testament to leading senior citizen aerobics classes.
>
> "What is bug spray, anyway?" he asked.

This is the second draft opening to *Tip A Canoe*. Since this is right at the beginning of the novel and I'm trying to grab hold of the reader's eyeballs, I decided that Dodee's description was too static, and yet I wanted the reader to know what she looked like because she's just as important to the story as Jim. So I broke it up for the final draft:

> "Bring bug spray?" Jim said.
>
> He glanced at his passenger, but Dodee Swisher kept her head of full soft

> curls, about the color of ripened wheat, buried in the information sheet on her lap.
>
> "What is bug spray, anyway?" he asked.
>
> She wore a light-blue jean shirt with red plaid showing at the collar and cuffs, cream colored denim pants, and soft loafers on her feet, her trim body a testament to leading senior citizen aerobics classes.

I tried to keep the reader hooked with the second question before completing Dodee's description. And I probably should have broken it up more, putting the bit about her trim body after the third question, but when I tried it, it didn't feel right. Maybe I'm splitting molehills here, to use a malapropism, and if it had been in a later chapter I might have left it, but this is the opening of the novel and I wanted to dare the reader to put it down.

If we don't grab for the quick and easy, the clichéd, but, like a vintner pressing juice from a grape, squeeze each word for meaning on many levels, we can Place our readers in the scene, include the props and information we need, use it to reflect our characters, and set the mood for what is happening, all without our readers hardly realizing it. Yet subliminally it will make the difference between them reading about a castle, or freezing their buns off in a drafty old Keep while the wind howls outside; the difference between them being informed about the stories of old bards, or warming their hands by a desert campfire as an ancient teller-of-tales stands under the stars and spins his magic.

Surprisingly often, writers seem to give no thought whatsoever to where the action of a story is to take place. Instead of imagining a complete context with solid ground for their people to walk on, they content themselves with putting a character in motion who can only perish from a lack of breathable air. Setting is a story's life-support system, and without it everything dies.

—Ben Nyberg, from "Why Stories Fail"

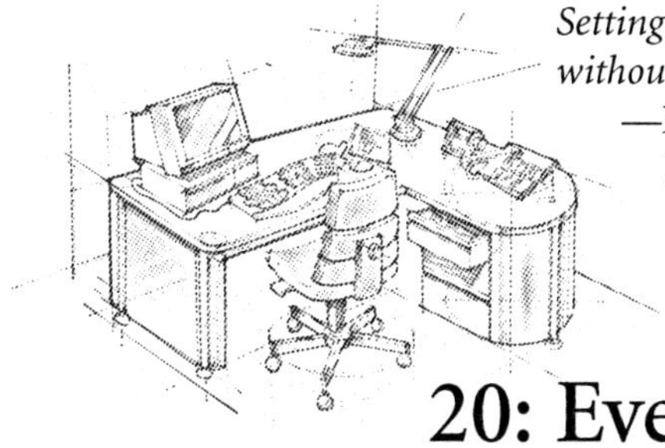

20: Everything Has a Time and Location

Locus

In Place we talked about the need to set our readers in the scene, to give them that sense of being there. We also need to give them the locus of events. The setting, the time, the season; the *where* and *when* of who, what, where, when, why, and how. We can brute force the locus:

> Oself sat in a taxi on a hot, muggy, late evening in Washington, D.C., in the summer.

Or we can finesse it by weaving it into the story.

> Oself sat in the open door of the taxi, feet on the cobblestone street, try-

> ing to figure out if he was going to throw up or not.
>
> A screaming whine split the air as an airliner, flashing red against an aluminum underbelly, zoomed in over Georgetown University four blocks to the west, raced overhead a second later, and flew off to wind its way down the Potomac corridor between the White House and the Pentagon.
>
> Out of desperation, Oself scanned the night sky for the three bright stars of Orion's belt, but if they were there, they were hidden by the glare of street lamps reflecting off the city's summer haze, an acrid aftertaste of auto exhausts and diesel busses and spent jet fuel.

Obviously you know which one I recommend. Again, it takes more words, but it rolls along like a movie. In fact, if we were film buffs, we could see both these descriptions in the evolution of the industry. Early movies often did a brute force fade-in at the beginning with printing telling us the place and time before going into the action. Movies today finesse the *where* by picturing landmarks, and the *when* by showing machinery and clothing. The exceptions to this are science fiction, where time and space can be wild, and in military stories, where a message's date-time-group is flashed across the screen, but even here I think finessing it is the better choice if the writer can pull it off.

Oh, yes, and for those smarty-pants who caught it, in the above example there was a plot-setup reason for looking for Orion, even though it cannot be seen in Washington's summer skies.

Costumes and customs can also be used to set the story's locus:

> Oself stuck ten arrows in his quiver, threw his bow over his shoulder, and stepped out onto the street. He had to jump back when a rider uniformed in the King's Guard clopped down the cobbled stones on a massive steed, paused to nail a notice to a wooden placard, and set off again in the direction of London town. Oself joined the gathering crowd as the town crier called out the message for those who couldn't read.
>
> "Fornicate under command of the King, his Majesty, Henry the Eighth."

Hmmmm, seems like there is an acronym there.

I didn't actually show the dress of the man because I haven't researched it and this is only an example. The same could be done in China, the South Seas, or the heart of Africa.

Setting

In choosing a setting for our stories, we have a choice of anyplace in the world or pulling one out of our head.

I based the town in *Bloody Bonsai* on Stone Harbor, New Jersey, but because I couldn't remember its details, I made up the town of Bolder Harbor. The secret is, folks, I had misspelled "boulder." Damn spellchecker. Rather than go back through the book or look completely stupid, I decided to use it to foreshadow the future in a negative way by giving the town a motto—"Bolder Harbor, where boldness is our vision and violence is unknown."

The point is, if we are going to describe a real place, I don't care if it's a burg on the mouth of New Guinea's Fly River, someone will have been there. I once mentioned on-line the comparison I used in chapter five: if you compare the population of No Trees, Texas, to New York City, you'd have the ratio of publishable first drafts to those that are not. Well, folks, No Trees, Texas is a spot on the road somewhere between Midland and New Mexico, and damn if someone out there in Internet Land didn't live twenty-five miles away from it.

If we describe a real place, we better get the details right. Screw them up and we lose credibility. We could also lose readers.

Also, if you describe a real setting, nothing beats standing in the place and slapping your eyeballs on it. If your character is walking along "P" Street outside Georgetown University in Washington, D.C., and you know it has an uneven brick sidewalk, put it in. Everything doesn't have to be real, but these things will give the story the taste of reality.

I've read books where it's obvious the author has never been in the place, only looked up a few street names on the map and threw in an odd detail to fake it. If we keep it sketchy so no one can find fault, we may get by, but if we can't actually be there, at least search out photos and do research. We owe our readers that much. Of course, if our setting is of a different time period, we have to do the research, in spades.

Since using real settings can get us into trouble, why not always make them up? Ed McBain does it in his 87th Precinct series.

Two reasons. People like to read about places where they live, visited, or hope to visit. This might be just the incentive for them to pick our book off the shelf and give it a look. Secondly, using real places helps to ground the story in reality. Even if we don't use a real place, we can still ground the story by tying it to a real place. The fictitious Bolder Harbor is north of Cape May and south of Stone Harbor, both real places.

But whether real or fictitious, we have to be consistent.

When I made up the town of Bolder Harbor, I drew a rough map of the town and referred to it whenever I moved characters around. In a still-hoped-to-be-published novel, I drew up a rough floor plan of a fictitious manor house. I spent pages describing for myself the wings, bedrooms, hallways, public rooms and kitchen. If I had presented it that way it would have been boring and too much detail to remember, but I used it for reference whenever my POV character was there. Everyone who read that story commented on how obvious it was that I had lived in that house.

We should treat our settings as we do our characters, even to the point of profiling them. You may pooh pooh the idea, but it works. Whatever we do to make our made-up places and scenes more real to us will make them more real to our readers.

Time

Above, we mentioned the need to establish the time of the story, but time must also pass during the story. The changing of the seasons can accomplish this, as well as day and night if the story is shorter, but it can also be much simpler—Oself kept the Wednesday appointment.

The main thing is to make sure all the times are consistent. If we say we will sail in five days on Sunday, we can't have the boat leaving Wednesday. If we want to show a scene that takes place during a finite time, we have to make the action reasonable for that time to pass:

> "We have to leave in two hours," Sam said.
>
> "In that case, I'll have another drink," Oself said, pouring from a bottle of Jack.
>
> "It's been one heck of a day."
>
> "It sure has."
>
> "Well," Sam said, looking at his watch, "drink up, it's time to go."
>
> "Already?" Oself finished off his drink. "Seems like only minutes ago you mentioned two hours."

This is exaggerated, of course, but the example holds. I don't think the time has to be exact, but enough has to happen to make the time of the scene plausible, that is, if a finite time is integral to the scene. Otherwise we can just say, "they dawdled until it was time to go."

Locus, time, and setting, like everything else in fiction, should blend into plot and dialogue and characterization to flavor it like salt and pepper on a steak.

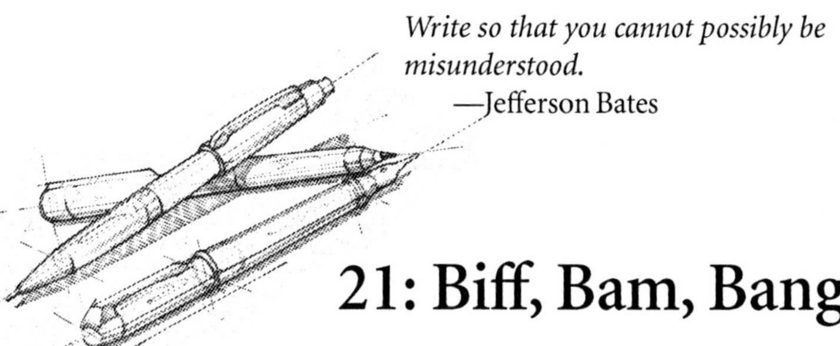

Write so that you cannot possibly be misunderstood.

—Jefferson Bates

21: Biff, Bam, Bang

The first step in writing action is to decide if we need it. If it doesn't add to the story, cut it. The second is to simplify. Instead of explaining all the steps of logging onto a computer—coming into the room, turning it on, sitting down, adjusting the chair, putting hands on keyboard, moving the mouse to a word processor program and clicking on it—can't we get by with: he flipped on the computer and brought up the word processor?

When most readers open up a novel, they want to step out of their everyday world and fantasize a bit, step into a fuller life, or at least a different one.

What they don't want is a lively treatise on chicken molting.

So we can come up with another couple of principles:

> No writer has a right to bore his readers.
> If we bore them, we'll lose them.

No big surprise there.

But what we might not realize is that when we confuse them, we'll bore them. Or to put it more simply:

> If we confuse them, we'll lose them.

So the third step is to clarify the action.

Clarity

If our writing is so muddled that our reader doesn't know what is going on, if he has to reread it a few times to figure it out, we might just as well write one boring sentence after another.

Effective writing is clear and concise. We should strive to keep our readers flowing over our words without a pause or stumble to break the dream.

On the other hand, if we go into a lengthy explanation of a critical action or story detail, we'll lose spontaneity and risk our readers nodding off.

So the first thing we have to do is to visualize the action, any action, in our minds. Maybe even walk it through. If it's vague in our minds, it will be vague on paper.

Next we put it all down, everything, bloated into boredom, to make sure there's no disputing what we have on paper. Then we work on it: eliminate everything that will muddy the picture, replace weak verbs for strong ones, use single words that will carry for two and operate on many levels, and rearrange sentence placement for impact and immediacy.

What's the difference between spending so many words that we bore the reader, or so few that we confuse them?

I'm still struggling with that. I think it's a judgement call every time.

Writing Action

Treat any action like you're trying to explain it to someone from Mars and you can't be far wrong.

If someone is behind a pane of thick glass trying to talk to Oself, our readers have to see it as Oself would, part pantomime, part hand signals, lip action and body language taking the place of speech. All of this could be confusing to Oself, and therefore to our readers, but the action has to be clear enough so that when the person comes from behind the glass and explains, it all falls into place. Tricky stuff.

The same thing goes for cutting meat at a dinner table. Seems like a simple process. But if a person does it in an unusual way, we better make clear what he is doing, and if this requires a couple of paragraphs, we better break it up with bits of action or conversation.

> John's chubby hands pared the fat off his steak with all the skill of a surgeon dissecting a frog. "I told her when she came to me," he said above the restaurant clatter, "I could not do anything for her."
>
> Oself held out his hands in a palms-up shrug. "So you let her just walk out into the rain?"
>
> "It was not my business."
>
> "Maybe not, but sending her out into the rain?" He watched John slice the remaining steak into precise one-inch strips, and he had the image of the frog being clinically dismembered. "Why didn't you call me?"
>
> John twisted the plate ninety degrees on the white tablecloth, eyes intent upon his operation. "I told you, it was not my business." Now he repeated the precision cuts crosswise through the strips, deftly cubing the frog into one-

> inch squares. "I did not want to get involved."
>
> "Well, screw you, John. I wouldn't practice my speech for the humanitarian award."
>
> Oself left him there, squatting on his chair, eyes bugging out in pleasure as he stabbed bits of meat and placed them between fat lips onto a long pink tongue.

This is just to show another way of doing it. If I did it right, we should be able to see John cutting the meat and a whole lot more. We have an example of dialogue, don't we? And characterization. We get a solid glimpse of what John is like. Notice that his actions are reflected in his dialogue, precise and without contractions. Notice also the "chubby" hands carving the "fat" off to give the impression that John has a few extra pounds on his frame. In the same way, I had him twist the plate on a white tablecloth and used "operation" to reinforce the idea of a surgical dissecting. I threw in the frog business to try to leave the reader with the impression of a toad catching flies. Don't know if that came off, but it's just a quickie to show some of the things that can be done. You could also say the white tablecloth didn't work either, but it was worth spending the two words. Finally, there is no telling here. Emphasis is placed on letting the eyes visualize everything.

The idea is to show how we can wrap dialogue and action and description and characterization and plot around one another to build the picture for our readers. We must always be ready to try different ways to bring a scene alive.

But suppose, folks, the above paragraphs add nothing to the book. Say we rewrite as we go, and it took us a lot of work to get it right, and at the end neither John nor the conversation adds anything to the story. We cut it out. We're not in the business of building elegant scenes, we're in the business of telling a story. Let me rephrase that. We're in the business of dramatizing a story.

In writing violent action we need to worry about pace as well as clarity.

> Stagman, gun steady, wiggled the fingers of his free hand. "I'll take the diamond now."
>
> Oself nodded.
>
> He might be about to get himself killed, but what other choice did he have? He only hoped Stagman was just as much of an amateur as he, except, of course, the guy had a forty-five.
>
> He pulled out the 54-carat stone and tossed it, twirling in the air, buoyed as a kite by the wind, sun popping off its many facets like Chinese fireworks, high and wide and just out of reach.
>
> Stagman suckered for it.
>
> And Oslef charged in right behind.
>
> Head down. Arms out. Legs churning. He smashed into the guy's gut. Drove him back. But the sonofabitch refused to go down.
>
> Then the world crashed onto the back of Oself's head.

Okay, so a 54-carat diamond is a bit much, along with buoyed like a kite, but what I'm trying to do is to stretch the time out here, like a slow motion camera, so that what follows will seem like hammer drills, bam, bam, bam. Short paragraphs, short sentences, pieces of sentences, give us a staccato immediacy. Then

I lengthened it out again to give the impression it all slowed down at the end.

Two other things to notice here.

If I had Oself just toss the stone and charge right in, the reader could wonder where that action came from, especially if it was out of Oself's normal character. So I had to let them know why Oself took this desperate action, and I did this by a bit of interior monologue. But I didn't say *Oself thought*, or worse, *Oself thought to himself*, instead I juxtaposed Oself's body language with the interior monologue to leave no doubt who was doing the thinking.

Also, I don't think "suckered" is a word, but is there any doubt what's happening? Sometimes stretching a word will give the most impact. But what gives it the impact is the sentence that leads into it. This is how I first wrote the paragraph:

> He pulled out the 54-carat stone and tossed it, high and wide, just out of reach, twirling in the air, buoyed as a kite by the wind, sun popping off its many facets like Chinese fireworks.
>
> Stagman suckered for it.
>
> And Oslef charged in right behind.

Can you see where this leaves a bit of ambiguity in the reader's mind? We're not sure what Stagman suckered for, and not knowing that, we wonder why Oself charged. But by rearranging the order to bring "high and wide and just out of reach" to the end of the sentence, it leads right into the following paragraph. Also by replacing the comma in "high and wide, just out of reach" with an "and" we slow the pace of it which we were trying to do for this paragraph.

A lot to think about, right?

Certainly too much for the first time we write it.

I must have rewritten that piece of action six or eight times for *Bloody Bonsai*, then changed the names to make it meaningful for this book and rewrote it three or four times here.

Why am I telling you this?

Because between the time I wrote that book and now, I've come to have a better understanding of how I'm trying to show things. It doesn't happen all at once. As we try to keep in our minds all the little techniques that will build our action, we will learn from rewrite to rewrite, and from book to book.

Don't be discouraged.

The secret of fiction writing is not being afraid to write something badly, and then rewriting it into a work of art.

We start out life with a lot of options but as we get down the road things close down, until at the end we have a narrow track. A book is the same, except in a book we can always go back and redo the beginning.

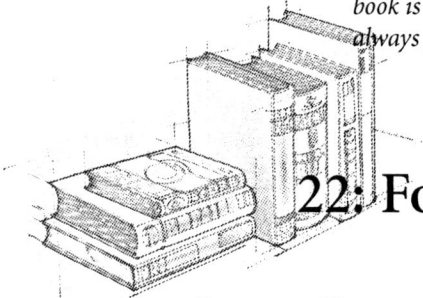

22: Foretelling

Setups and Payoffs

Some writers and teachers call this foretelling, but I prefer setups and payoffs because it tells us we must prepare our readers to accept an action that would otherwise be a bolt out of left field.

Or is it, "out of the blue?"

I got to keep my clichés straight.

The success of any story depends on the finesse with which the author sets up each payoff:

> Marsha felt her head slam against the butcher-block island as John bent her back across it. She had always liked that feature in her kitchen. His body pressed her down. Fear gripped her as she knew from past newspaper articles that he was intent on brutally murdering her. As he grabbed her around the neck, smashing her head against the counter, she fought to hold on and suddenly remembered the ten-inch chef's knife she kept at the side of the island to cut vegetables. Desperately she reached around for it. She felt

> the handle, gripped it, plunged the blade
> into John's neck.

What's the trouble with this?

We have to take the time to show the reader there is a butcher-block island in the kitchen, that past newspaper articles indicate John will kill her, and *suddenly* she remembers a knife is there when she desperately needs it.

All this stops the action and stretches credibility. It gives the reader the feel of being made up as the writer goes along, which, of course, it is. That's why it's called fiction. But we don't want to broadcast this to our readers like a blinking red sign; we want everything to flow like it's real and happening before their very eyes.

So how would we do that?

The rule of setups and payoffs is to setup something twice if it's subtle, the second time in case the reader missed it, or once if it's a *big* show, before playing it out in a payoff.

Suppose, for the above example, in chapter two we setup Marsha talking to her lover while cutting vegetables for dinner on the butcher-block, and when she finishes she wipes the chef's knife and slips it into a holder at the side. Now the reader knows there's a butcher-block island in the kitchen and a knife in its side holder. But the action is on making dinner and they may miss it. So in chapter eight, she admonishes her son for using the chef's knife in the living room to cut string, and she returns it to the butcher-block. Then we work out a similar scenario for the newspaper articles, not that John is the killer, but someone is bumping people off. Say this is splashed across the headlines and Marsha makes a big thing of it with her friends, so we only have to mention this once.

With everything now set up, let's see how it plays:

> Marsha felt her head slam against the butcher-block island as John bent her back across it, his body pressing her down. He would kill her. That certainty flashed in her mind as she groped for a weapon. He smashed her head down again. She fought to hold on, and then felt the handle of her chef's knife in the side holder. She grabbed it in one fluid motion and plunged it into John's neck.
>
> Adios, John.

See how much faster the motion flows?

That last sentence I just threw in.

My problem in the past has been, if mentioning something twice was good, mentioning it three or twenty-three times had to be better. No, folks, that's telegraphing it, like saying—look, nudge nudge, knife. Over-setting-up is as much a problem as not setting-up.

It also leads to over-writing, of which I have also been guilty. The only negative review of *Bloody Bonsai* mentioned that I used "cornflower-blue eyes" eight times in the book. I started out using it twenty times and so thought cutting back to eight was an accomplishment, but perhaps I should have cut it below that. I've taken note for future novels.

If we want our story to flow seamlessly, we'll not only use setups and payoffs for major things, like the chef's knife above, but for minor events as well.

Way back when we talked about first drafts, I mentioned that we better keep notes of the things we'll need to go back and change. If in chapter thirty, we find we need our hero to make a fast getaway, we better go back and mention he owns a Ferrari. That's a setup. We better not only imply he owns a Ferrari, but that he knows how to use it. In chapter three, we show Oself slam a red Ferrari into a controlled skid, stop in front of a restaurant, go inside. If we make it elaborate enough, that's all we need. But it wouldn't hurt to show him gassing it up, or cleaning the windshield. Now when Oself has to get the heck away from some bad guys, nobody's surprised when he jumps over the low slung door, jams the key in the ignition, and slams the pedal to the floor, spitting dust and sand and pebbles as he shoots off into the night.

Suppose in chapter thirty-eight we decide that the restaurant in chapter three, where Oself went into a controlled skid, needs to have a cocktail lounge for meeting with the police on neutral turf. I could say, "They walked into a bar in La Fonda Restaurant that they hadn't seen before." I might get by, but it's sloppy and contrived, and it wouldn't flow smoothly. Our reader wonders how come Oself didn't know it was there. Is he stupid? But if I go back and have Oself glance in at the cocktail lounge as he walks to a table, and if later on he passes though the bar on his way to the restroom, when he walks in for that chapter thirty-eight meeting, our readers will ease on in without a blink.

We can also use negative setups.

Suppose we want to kill a governor or a movie star in chapter twenty-five. We want it to be a surprise and yet have the reader prepared for it. In chapter two or three we have Oself say, "He has so many bodyguards around, who would be dumb enough to try to get an autograph, much less harm him?" Then in chapter six someone asks Oself, "He has a bunch of bodyguards around, but would any take a bullet for him?" And Oself replies, "With that many bruisers around, no one would be stupid enough to try to shoot." And our reader says, "Hmmm, oh, yeah." But we are just nicking their suspicions and by chapter twenty-five it's slipped out of their consciousness. So, bang-bang, one dead movie star and one surprised reader, yet, because of the negative setup, it's not coming out of a blue bolt of lightning in left field.

We can do anything if we set it up properly.

We'll talk more about this in the next chapter on story logic, but for now let's go back to Oself making a getaway in a red Ferrari. What if Oself hardly has money for food, much less own a car? How could he drive off in a red Ferrari?

Suppose in chapter one we have him living in a rich friend's guesthouse, say on a tropical island, like Hawaii. And since Oself is a struggling detective, in chapter two the rich friend says that while he's away Oself can use the Ferrari if he keeps an eye on the estate. Now would he be able jump into the red Ferrari and make that getaway? And can you say, *Magnum P.I.*?

Want a perfect example of setups and payoffs?

Rent *Medicine Man* with Sean Connery.

I recommend this movie to every novice writer I know, but almost no one goes through the trouble of getting it.

Watch the movie once to see how well it works for entertainment. Everything flows. Then watch it a second time with a pad and pencil and mark down every event that takes place, even minor things from the opening scene of burning trees. I could go on and on and list one thing after another, but that would spoil the movie and keep you from ferreting these things out for yourself. You'll learn from this. Nothing is left to chance. Each event is subtly shown, shown again, setting up the viewer to be ready for everything as it's finally paid off.

From the beginning we've stressed "easy reading is hard writing." If we make an effort to setup every payoff, we'll scoop up our readers and carry them along in the moment, without any bumps in the road to shake them out of the enjoyment of an easy read.

Man occasionally stumbles over the truth. Then he picks himself up, dusts himself off, and proceeds as though nothing has happened.

—Attributed to Ben Franklin

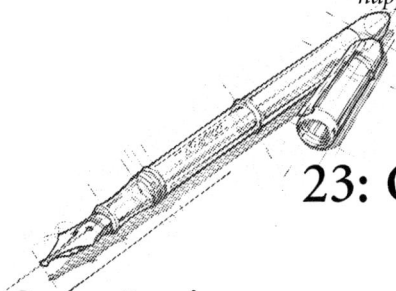

23: Credibility

Story Logic

It's crazy to even have to take up this subject. Why would we write something illogical?

> The killer fired his forty-five, but quick thinking Oself caught the bullet in his teeth.

Oh, yeah, that works.

We can see obvious flaws like this, but how about something more subtle?

In *Killing Thyme*, good old James Dandy runs out of his hotel when he hears the sound of an accident and crawls to someone under a truck. My editor, Dorrie O'Brien, wanted to know why would he do that. Jim Dandy is a physical therapist and, being a healer, I thought it would be an obvious thing for him to do, but if she didn't get it, you can bet my readers wouldn't. I went back in earlier chapters setting up that he's also a volunteer EMT, emergency medical technician. Now there is no longer any doubt why he rushed to someone's aid.

In *Total Control* by David Baldacci, a super-smart woman lawyer comes upon the guy who killed her husband and is trying to kill her. There is a struggle, the bad guy gets knocked out, and the lawyer stands over him with gun in hand. Does she tie the guy up, call the police, shoot him dead, or leave him talking in a high voice? No, she runs from the house so the guy can come after her again. Give—me—a—break. This might be convenient for the plot, but is it logical for real life? A ditzy broad might do it, but a tough-as-nails, think-on-your-feet corporate lawyer? Will I journey with this author again? I was told *Absolute Power* was a much better book so I read it. Guess what? This time it was a male tough-as-nails, think-on-your-feet corporate lawyer, standing above a bad guy he had just body slammed onto a concrete subway platform. Does he tie the guy up, call the police, shoot him dead, or leave him talking in a high voice? He not only runs away, but, two blocks down the road, suddenly remembers he left the evidence that can clear him of murder back on the pavement with the knocked-out bad guy. *Now* ask me if I'll journey with this author again?

I bring up this example because once we lose credibility with our readers, we've lost them. All fiction crosses a line where the reader has to be willing to suspend belief. Who really thinks Miss Marple comes upon a new murder every week? Or Jim Dandy and Dodee Swisher find a body every time they go on an Elderhostel? But once these opening conditions are accepted, everything else had better ring true if we want to maintain our credibility and keep our readers.

Still, Baldacci sold a passel of books. Go figure.

Rob Pegoraro, in reviewing a mystery in Washington Post's *Book World*, complained once about "the most annoying of clichés, The Girl Too Scared to Pull the Trigger." All clichés rob our writing of spontaneity, and many times of its believability. I'm betting that because we've all read about bad things happening to the girl who doesn't pull the trigger, a real-life modern woman will blast the ass of a guy hell-bent on doing her harm, and then blow smoke from the gun barrel after doing so.

But these things creep in. Sometimes we get so close to our work we don't see the obvious.

In one of my stories I had a man working up an elaborate plan to steal a book. When I showed it to a friend who does editorial work for me, he asked me why not just buy the book. Well, the book cost over half a million. I knew that. But I had failed to let the reader know that.

In an otherwise good book—*Dead Eyes*, by Stuart Woods—a police detective is searching for a stalker who has recently moved, but when he thinks he has tracked down the stalker's new residence, he never asks the neighbors if the man had recently moved in. It was integral to the story, but either he didn't see the obvious, or he ignored standard police procedure because it would have screwed up his plot.

Do this often and we'll lose credibility.

I once talked to a writer from the Great Lakes area who told me how his character took off in a private plane for another city and fifteen minutes out found a bomb in the plane that was set to go off in fifteen minutes. This was supposed to be some great piece of suspense in getting back to the airport before the bomb went off. I asked him how come they just didn't land on a road and walk away. He didn't want to hear that. It ruined the plot.

Real-world logic must never be bent to satisfy plot. Plot must always be bent to follow real-world logic. In *Dead Eyes*, setting the house in the boonies would have eliminated neighbors. In the private plane scenario, if they had flown out over one of the Great Lakes, there would have been no roads to land on.

If we need to create an illogical situation, then we need to setup a logical reason why the illogical situation came about. In *Dead Eyes*, if we couldn't put the house in the boonies, how about a big community party so the neighbors wouldn't be home? Stretching, but logical. The woman who couldn't pull the trigger? How about making her a Quaker? Or when she was a girl she shot and killed her father? Both logical reasons why she might now hesitate to shoot a guy coming after her.

We can do anything if we set it up properly.

Want our hero to suddenly break into a warehouse and save the damsel in distress at the last moment? Don't give us a miraculous coincidence; in fiction, coincidence must always work against our hero. Instead, go back in the story and set up a logical reason for him to show up there.

Want to have a killer be some strange gargoyle with mysterious powers? Pop four moons up in the sky and we're immediately alerted to the fact that a different standard of logic must apply. Now we can do most anything. But once we establish that off-world logic we better follow through with it for the rest of the story.

So how can we have a surprise ending then?

It, too, must be logical within the story's conditions. A satisfying surprise has its seeds sown so skillfully that only after the trap is sprung can the reader go back and pick them out. A good mystery has the same construction. Mystery readers must be able to either glory in the fact they figured out the killer, or be able to go back and pick out clues they missed. For a perfect example of this, check out the movie *Sixth Sense.* Its powerful surprise ending reflects the action that has taken place and leaves the viewer satisfied.

Fiction writing is not a series of isolated functions. Setups and payoffs are woven into dialogue which is woven into dramatize-not-inform and POV and plot and characterization and effective writing, but for it to be believable, the whole structure must rest on a bedrock of logic. Our readers already know the story is fiction. If we make it implausible as well, the whole make-believe world crumbles like sand castles before the sea.

Research

Like logic, our research has to be correct. If we say Oself eased off the safety on his revolver, we've probably just lost a bunch of readers because there ain't no safety on a revolver.

I avoid research whenever I can, but if I'm using a real description, like we mentioned in Place, then I better make damn sure it's correct. The same if I do something with a computer or wear a certain type of pants. If I wear a police vest, it behooves me to know who manufactured it, what it feels like, or its color. That's if I want to use them.

The other thing is to wait until we've finished the first draft before we do our research. I know, I know, for some people research is what gets them into the story. If you are one of those people, go for it.

The problem with doing the research first is that we will probably do more research than is necessary. And with all the good stuff we collected through sweat and tears, we'll be trying to figure someway to cram it in.

By waiting until we've completed our first draft we cut down on the amount of research, and lose the temptation to stuff something in just because it took so much work to find it.

Being a full-time writer is kind of like jumping off a cliff only to discover if you can fly...and then realizing you can never land. The flying is great, but man, those arms do ache.

—Neal Shusterman

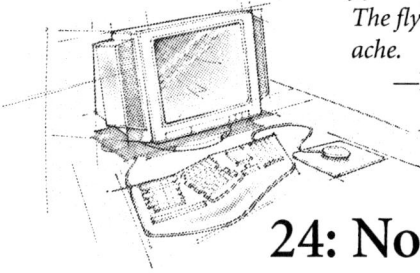

24: No Rest for the Weary

What is the difference between conflict, tension, and suspense?

When I attended college, seventeen million years ago, whenever I went out for a few drinks or on a date, I always had a constant, droning voice whispering in my mind that I should be studying. Had my mental ears been better, no doubt I would have been a straight "A" student then and a millionaire now.

Oh, yeah.

But the underlying *tension* was always that I should be studying, the *conflict* was that I wanted to party, and the *suspense*...which would prevail.

Tension

Tension in a novel is our opening premise. We are accused of murder; our lover wants to dump us; we are about to be fired. How do we handle that? This is the opening question that drives the story through to its climax. Other questions may and should arise. Will our spouses leave us; will the tension screw up our stomachs; will a change in water give us diarrhea? These too may be answered along the way. But the underlying tension is always there. There may be brief interludes—love scenes and watching sunsets—when things ease off, but there must always be that dog prowling along in the background with a tenacious gait.

> The loon lay on a sun-bleached dock. The way its neck hung flaccidly over the side made it look obscene. Sally searched the shuttered houses that lined the mottled lake for signs of life. Nothing. Nor in the low, lead-gray sky. Only the wind, whistling through skeletal trees like a plaintive funeral dirge, broke the silence.
>
> But something had placed the loon there.
>
> Something to think about on cold nights.

There is tension in the dead loon and the search for life on the mottled lake. It's echoed in the undressed trees, plaintive funeral dirge of the wind, and the houses shuttered against her. The question is, something stalked the loon, and maybe is stalking the female narrator. These could be metaphors, say in a literary novel, for events in her life, or her state of mind, or for things to come. It can also border on suspense if the terror stalking her turned out to be real. The more she comes back to the lake, physically or mentally, the more we'll increase that tension.

The amount of tension also defines the genre. Action and thriller novels have a high level of tension built into them.

An excellent example is *Nathan's Run* by John Gilstrap. He starts off with police searching for a young escapee from prison accused of murder. We switch to the escapee, who is just a boy, and who is innocent. Another switch to some background players who are trying to kill the boy without us knowing why. That's the tension line—the boy trying to stay alive—and although it eases at times as other events take place, the killers trying to wipe him out, the police trying to capture him, it relentlessly drives the story to its conclusion.

In mystery novels, someone committed a crime and everything is ultimately focused on catching the perpetrator. Ratchet this down, slow the pace, and it becomes a cozy.

Eliminate the tension, and you eliminate the need to be read. Do it before the end, and it *is* the end.

Conflict

Conflict is that which opposes our protagonist, in every scene, from bringing the novel's original question to a resolution. This could range from something major—our cliché traffic jam keeping us from preventing a murder—to something relatively mild like a misunderstanding. They must be present in every scene or nothing is happening. All dialogue must contain conflict, however gentle, just in the give and take of conversation.

> "Bring bug spray?" Jim asked, powering his blue Lincoln down Interstate 95.
>
> He glanced at his passenger, but Dodee Swisher kept her head of full soft curls buried in the information sheet on her lap.
>
> "What is bug spray, anyway? Like window spray to make the bugs clean? Hair spray to make them stiff?" He turned down his lips and nodded. "Now stiff

> might work. If you wanted to conjure up a really fun Elderhostel week, you'd say, 'bring genital spray.'" He glanced at her again. "Right?"
>
> "I'm not touching that."
>
> "The trouble with spray is it covers everything. Pan spray to make pans slick. House spray to make rooms smell nice. WD-40 spray to loosen nuts." He grinned. "Probably not something you want in a genital spray."
>
> "Repellent."
>
> "Damn right it would be repellent."
>
> "Bug"—she let it hang in the air a moment—"repellent."
>
> "Oh, that sounds a whole lot better. Bring bug repellent. Does that sound like more fun?"
>
> She lifted her head and her cornflower blue eyes riveted him with points of steel. "How does 'single rooms' sound?"

These guys are not ready to get into fisticuffs, but we do have conflict, and Jim's grousing is about to get him into major trouble.

There is also conflict that comes about just because of our imperfect form of communication, which in turn brings about misunderstanding.

> "What's the big deal about calling and letting me know if you're going to be home for dinner?" Sally asked.

"I'll be home," Oself answered. "Just take it for granted."

"I'd like you to call if I'm going to prepare a big dinner."

"Don't order me to call. If I want to call—"

"What's the big deal, sweetheart?"

He shook his head, clamping down so hard on his jaw his teeth ached, and he glared at her. "That's just something like my stepmother would say."

Sally's mouth dropped open.

He let out a breath and shrugged. "When I would come home, there was never much to eat. But if I didn't come home, oh wow, she had spent all afternoon over a hot stove fixing a fantastic meal. Or if I called to say I wouldn't be home, then it was, 'well, all right, I have this big meal planned, but I guess I'll have to forget it now.' Damned if I'll ever live like that again."

Every scene and bit of dialogue needs conflict, but that doesn't mean it has to be adversarial. There's conflict just in exchanging ideas, trying to find out what the other is thinking.

She folded her hands on the desk. "I thought I might hear from you yesterday."

"I wasn't here yesterday."

Her left eyebrow arched.

Oself smiled and waited her out.

"You weren't here? You mean in the building? In the city, in Maryland or Virginia, the eastern seaboard? What?"

"I wasn't here, not in the city, or Maryland or Virginia, the eastern seaboard, not even in the country or the decade."

Now both eyebrows arched. "This is going to be a long story, right?" She picked up a pencil and rolled it between the flat palms of her hands. "Oself, if this is some kind of a ploy"—the eyes leveled on him—"like coming onto me..."

He took a deep breath and eased it out. "Do you want to hear this?"

"Depends. As your friend, okay. But not as your psychologist."

"How about a friend who's a psychologist, like I might ask a friend who's a mechanic what he thinks the ping in my engine is."

She studied him for a moment, then nodded.

There's hardly anything adversarial here, but the exchange of information is like batting a ping-pong ball back and forth across a net. One side walks away and the game is over. But it doesn't work if they're both on the same side of the net.

If we show Oself sitting down on a porch and closing his eyes to rest, there may be conflict if he should be somewhere else. But if not and I go on with it for a few paragraphs—Oself is still sleeping, a nice sleep, a warm sleep, deep down, nothing but out-to-lunch sleep, and he's still sleeping—guess how long we'll be able to get away with that?

But suppose he closes his eyes because he hadn't any sleep, and he needs to sleep because he has to get up in two hours, and he can't sleep because his head is full of the day's events. Ah, now we have conflict, even if it's only in his mind, and our readers will hang in there because the conflict itself provides action.

And then there's suspense.

There's always suspense.

Even in a slow novel there's always the question of whether and how our original premise will be solved. But when we normally talk about suspense in writing, we're not talking about how some esoteric question will be resolved, we're talking about nail-biting, edge-of-our-chair suspense that increases in intensity as the novel or scene paces along.

What we're really talking about is how to build suspense, which is the subject of the next chapter.

See how nifty I set you up to lead right into the next chapter?

Oh, yeah.

There has to be conflict. And until the conflict is resolved there is tension, because of the conflict. People in conflict with each other, people in conflict with society, their government, philosophically, politically, socially. There is conflict and conflict produces tension. And the solution to the problem releases tension and that is probably when the play should end.

—Edward Albee, from "On Playwriting," *Dramatics* magazine

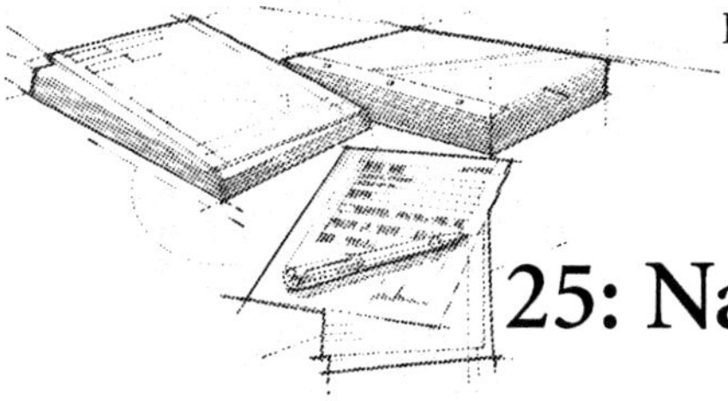

25: Nail Biting

Suspense

How do we build suspense in a novel?

First we have to make sure everything is set up. If you haven't read the chapter on setups and payoffs, read it first because suspense will be lost if it's not set up. We can't intersperse action with explanation without losing spontaneity. Even writing another complete scene is better than trying to insert things at the last minute.

> Oself pulled out a gun, *which he happened to remember he kept in a cabinet under the sink, given to him three weeks ago by his brother, and he hid it there to keep it from his children*, and pointed it at the killer.

If we haven't seen the gun before, we have to know where it came from, how it happened to be there, all of this stuff. But if we had already set up our readers by showing Oself getting the gun and hiding it under the sink, we could leave out all the stuff in italics. See how fast it would read then without missing a beat?

So, setups-and-payoffs out of the way, we turn to ways of tightening the screw till it is ready to snap. Just remember not to over-egg the custard, as the British say. Once the device becomes obvious, we'll lose both credibility and suspense.

Ticking Clock

If we have to defuse a bomb, the ticking down of a digital clock will lock us into the action taking place. The problem is, this has been so overdone it's become a cliché; on television shows it's as subtle as being bludgeoned with a hammer. Still, if done with finesse and subtlety, the ticking down of a digital clock still works.

But a ticking clock device doesn't have to be an actual clock. An airplane slowly running out of gas over the Great Lakes as Oself tries to coax it to an airport. A train running wild toward a crowded station and Oself trying to stop it. Remember the movie *Silver Streak*? Anything that signals the countdown of a finite time will work.

> Oself pushed on the door that had been slammed shut and now was apparently locked. Nothing he could do would make it budge. And to make matters worse, water started seeping up from a grate in the floor. He checked for cracks in the walls, someplace he could pry open

> enough to squeeze through, or even, as the level continued to rise, big enough to just drain off the water.

Carrying this on for the whole novel might be a bit much, but it could probably work for a scene or two. And if this closed space is not to our liking, how about water pouring into the hold of a ship as Oself battles to keep it afloat long enough to make landfall?

Oself notices water in the bilge early in the game, bails it out and later sees it again, no real problem yet, but it's always present, and as the weather worsens the hull-works and more water starts pouring in, things become critical as Oself has to bail and man the boat at the same time. Then we slowly tighten the screw as the weather worsens still, and perhaps he crashes into a floating log, until the battle is joined between the sea seeking the boat, and Oself fighting for her life, and his.

Stretching Time

Stretching time is the opposite of the ticking clock. Again, it requires subtlety. If we bring our hero into a dangerous climactic scene, we can stretch the suspense by describing the place, painting it very heavy or dark and foreboding.

> Oself sailed the little boat through the rain under storm jib alone, arms aching as he continued working the thump, thump of the pump, fighting to keep her afloat. The wind tore at his hat and drops of water stung his face like watery bees and left a salt taste on his lips. He

squinted toward the bow as the boat rode up on the crest of a wave. And stopped pumping. Frozen.

A mountain blotted out his horizon, a moving, churning, wall that lifted out of the ocean and reached for the sky. It sucked out the water before it, creating an endless trough. Oself's boat waddled waterlogged down into it and the apparition grew into a dark Matterhorn. A cliff face without hand holds. No place to drive pinions. No road to go around. And yet the brave boat's bow rose to the challenge. Up they started as the storm jib went slack. In the wall's wind shadow. Suddenly silent. The bow slowed, rising only by its buoyancy now.

And high above it, the first tumble of the monster's crest. They moved inside the curl and it sucked away his breath. Rising on the wave even as it looped over them, a shroud that consumed the daylight, like a roof covering the world, hanging there, suspended, unstable, black water laced with streaks of white foam racing down its face, folding over him, the boat standing on its stern, sliding backwards, Oself clutching the pump handle with a grip strong enough to bend the steel.

Then the ceiling rolled down on him, a dark malevolent cloud that roared like a banshee from hell.

Well, you get the picture. This is not meant to be a paragon of writing, but just to give us an idea of how we can stretch things out to increase the suspense. Remember to use the senses: see, hear, smell, touch, and taste.

Dean Koontz did a great job of stretching out a scene in *Ticktock* by simply describing a beast as it advanced on the hero, the eyes, the sounds, the way it moved, how it smelled, so that while one part of the reader's mind is absorbed in the details, the other is screaming for the hero to get the hell out of there.

Again, do it with finesse. Dramatize, don't inform. No eyes rolling—or filled—with horror. No clichés. And end it before it becomes obvious.

Skew the Normal

It sounds like an oath. Skew the Cowboys. Of course that would only be said by a Redskin's fan.

Write about a placid scene where everything is normal, but twist one thing out of place.

> Sally carried her laundry basket along the second floor hallway aglow in sunlight streaming through the west windows. She paused at three clown pictures hanging on the wall, studying them, pleased at the purchases she had picked up for two dollars at a yard sale. Not junk. Her years at the conservatory screamed of their quality, something reminiscent of Renoir or Monet or Sisley. She had unearthed a treasure, but how much they

> were worth would have to wait until she could get them appraised.
>
> What were they doing in a yard sale?
>
> Why had no one else picked them up?
>
> Sally glanced at her watch and scurried on. She would have to hurry if she wanted to reach the club in time for a pre-lunch cocktail. She turned into her bedroom, filled with the morning sun.

Okay, so you see it?

Actually there's a number of red flags here, but only one thing really out of place, vastly out of place.

If she's hurrying for a luncheon date, what's that glow streaming in the west windows? I also added the morning sun in the bedroom just to make sure you didn't think it was a screw up, but if we were writing for real, that might be overdoing it. Especially if this is the first setup. There's a difference between a subtle hint and overwriting. The first is trusting your readers' intelligence to not let it get by them, the second is that poke in the ribs—"D'ja get it?"

All else being the same, we could rejoice with Sally at her great purchase, but there are those nagging questions that leave us with an uneasy feeling. Something not quite right. The clincher is the sun business.

The next time we visit the clowns, what's that red smudge on one picture frame? And the following time, are they on the opposite wall? See? We could work it just as well with everything being perfectly normal, but the lights are on in the daytime. Then a picture askew. A window cracked. Each step tightening the screw.

Another way is to leave something out of a normal setting, something that would ordinarily be there and is not. No stove in the kitchen. No commode in the bathroom. And the thing doesn't have to be tangible.

> Sally walked through Harry's library and stopped mid-way, glancing around at the pale green walls she had helped paint, the curtains that she had helped pick out, and the hanging art work they had collected so lovingly over the years. She would have to box them up.
>
> But what had stopped her in mid-stride?
>
> She glanced around again, breath held, then exhaled in that vacant whisper of the place. An emptiness had taken hold and expanded to fill the air like a foul odor seeping up from a sewer pit.
>
> Harry had been in the grave—what?—less then twenty four hours. Yet the spirit of the house had fled. Which, of course, was ridiculous. The feel of a house is not an energy that can be snapped off with a switch.
>
> Can it?
>
> No. What had changed was only her perception.

Let's break this down. What had changed was Sally's perception. Or had it? We get tension from her stopping in mid-stride and holding her breath. Something's not quite right. Then there is the off-slant feeling by the use of a vacant whisper, and foul odor expanding to fill the air. Notice, none of these things are actually present in the room. It's the use of narrative description that gives us the uneasy feeling. Then the questions arise. If the spirit fled, what had taken its place? And we imply that it surely had by over emphasizing that it hadn't. Remember, we can negatively set things up by overstating the positive.

The Unknown

Okay, we talked about the ticking clock, stretching time, and skewing the normal. Now we take an unknown place and the things found there, then ratchet up the tension.

> Sally descended the deep stairwell into the castle's bowels, coming out on a raised platform. A long subterranean tunnel stretched before her; the platform's candles unable to penetrate the dusk of its arched ceiling. Torches along one side, ensconced in holders at twenty-foot intervals, sent shadows licking across the stone floor as they flickered in a breeze that ebbed and flowed and tasted of salt.
>
> Somewhere the passage connected with the sea.
>
> She stood in the platform's island of candlelight and stared down at the long row of torches. The shadows would make for slow going, but they aided her as well. If someone came the other way,

she could hide in them, or race back to the stairs.

She descended from the platform and started out, one foot after another, careful of falling. She reached the third torch before she paused, listening, aware that something had changed. She glanced back toward the platform only to see it had been swallowed by darkness. Not only had the candles burned out, but also the first torch, leaving only one behind.

Burned out or blown out?

She reached for the torch beside her, to illuminate the way back, but it hung too high. The next one looked lower and she strode toward it. Then stopped. Something had changed again. She jerked around in time to see the last two torches wink out. She hurried forward to the next torch, but again it was out of reach. And on to the next as the one behind puffed out, leaving only a black void where there had once been stairs.

If the others went out, she'd be trapped.

She rushed along the passage, but the next torch popped out even before she reached it, and then the next as she broke into a run, racing after the extinguishing lights to keep from getting caught in the blackness that stalked her as silently as a cat.

Weeell, you get the picture. You could scream cliché at me, a woman going into a dungeon alone, but I can scream back that she has a rational escape route set up so it's not really a cliché. Then as she moves along we start tightening the screw by cutting off her escape. At first it's one light, way back, then they start popping off closer to her, and finally blinking off in front of her so she has to race to catch up, driving Sally toward some unseen horror? And the reader right along with her?

In this example we used light as our driving force. But couldn't we use something else? How about the snakes in *Raiders of the Lost Ark*? Or the rats in *Indiana Jones and the Last Crusade*? Take notes when you're viewing movies. When Hollywood avoids the clichés to build tension, they do it right.

But couldn't we even use something that is completely innocuous?

> Red roses. What a lark when they first arrived. She held the stems where the thorns had been clipped off and smelled the petals' rich scent. Secret admirer? Someone from the office? Someone from the dancing class she was taking?
>
> That would be more like it.
>
> Dancing, dining, flowers.
>
> They went together.
>
> When the second dozen came it was even more intriguing, but when it reached twenty dozen in one day, coming at half hour intervals, from florists all over the city, thorns still on the stems, the sun had gone out of it. This was no longer just an admirer, secret or otherwise. Now the roses were hammer blows

> beating down the gates of her castle. When the bell rang again her patience broke and she yanked open the door to scream at the deliveryman.
>
> Only then did she realize her mistake.

You see. Of course all this is more like informing rather than dramatizing, but I'm trying to give you the idea of how to build suspense in a few paragraphs rather than actually writing the scenes.

Anything done with finesse can be used to build suspense.

You don't believe me?

I will not argue with you.

Just know that I have your address. And tonight, when you turn your light off, make sure all the windows are shut. And locked. How about the door? Did you remember to put the night latch on? And set the alarm?

Then you have nothing to worry about.

Unless?

Unless I am already inside. In a closet perhaps. Under a bed.

And maybe I'm a spirit-thing crammed into the top of an uncapped ballpoint pen. Waiting for you. Waiting for—No!

Don't put the cap on that pen or I'll *mmmmffttfmmmt*...

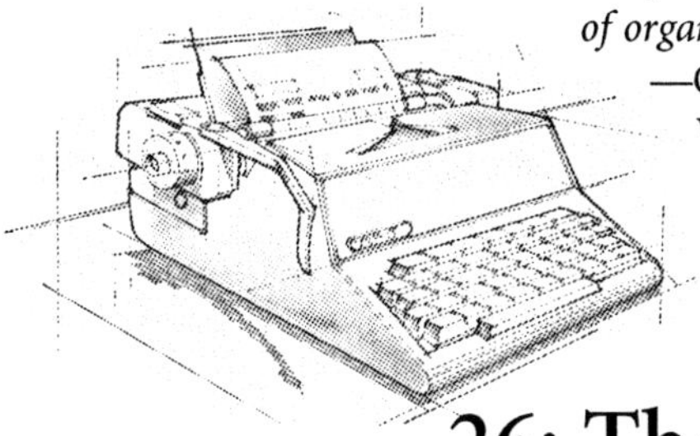

There is a foreground and a background of interest, and the writer should be careful to place each item in its proper location. Like unity and coherence, emphasis is a principle of organization.
—Cleanth Brooks and Robert Penn Warren

26: The Backs, Story & Flash

Back-Story

Back-story is similar to character background that we talked about in Character Profiles, but it's different in that it's the story before the actual story begins: when was the town founded; what was the name of the old high school; who played on the football team; whatever. Something we need to know, but it's not all used in the story.

Suppose we think we need a lot of back-story stuff up front in a novel in order to keep the chronology from getting screwed up. Put all the back-story stuff in. Lay it all out in your first draft. Don't worry if it's boring or not.

Just remember that's only for the first draft.

When we've finished it, we cut everything out of the back-story not absolutely needed for the fore-story. A lot of science fiction starts out giving us a chronology of future history so that the even more future story makes sense. But is it all unnecessary? Quick and dirty:

> Oself stood at the window port looking down on the dark side of the planet, to the lights of Mars Base Habitat 4. A box-shaped transporter drifted into view, preparatory to docking. Maybe he should head down and do some sightseeing before he answered the call for the new intergalactic war.

Once we see there's a dark side to a planet and know it's Mars, don't we slip right into the future? And being there, other things become possible because we are operating on future-logic. We know there's a war because Oself tells us in internal monologue, but do we need to know everything about it at this point? Why did it start? Who are the combatants? We can find that stuff out as we go along.

We don't want to clog up the beginning of a novel with a lot of facts. If we can get our readers involved in our story and caring about our characters, they will more readily wade through some boring facts later on. Some. But skin it down to the bare minimum.

Okay, suppose when we've finished our first draft we're still convinced we need a lot of back-story stuff up front. How do we handle it?

The best way is to reveal it while another piece of story action is going on. While our readers' concentration is on the action, we can slip in the necessary information:

> Oself sat in the lounge as he waited for Bork, watching a pretty blond woman on television's History Channel.

"The roots of the present war go back to ancient Europe during the malevolent Hitler period—"

"Hi," Bork said, plopping in the seat beside him, "sorry I'm late."

"—when the Nazis preached racial superiority."

Oself waved the apology aside. "You're here, that's what matters. Where can we get at the latest weaponry?"

Bork shrugged. "I know someone in ammo technology."

"—a group of these white supremacists set out to develop their own society halfway across the galaxy."

"Can you get hold of him?"

"I can sure try."

"—at the time, they passed out of history, only now to explode into the news as the New Universal Order, an empire to last for a thousand millennia."

Can we follow the above story segment? I think so. It doesn't have to be conversation, it could take place during a fight. Or a sex scene where we might play the history off the amorous action for amusing results. And it doesn't have to be television. Radio, tape recorder, a conversation between two other characters. How about two cops talking about a case during an autopsy—the autopsy grabbing our interest while the cops relate the case facts, or the other way around? Think back to where we've seen this in movies.

The danger here is we can't have Oself tell Bork something he should already know or the conversation will sound phony.

But if Oself is a visiting policeman from New York, it would be logical for L.A. cop Bork to fill him in. It could also be done while eating a steak dinner. How about setting up the first chapter with Oself in a classroom? While the teacher is giving a history lecture, young Oself's interest is in what's going on outside the window and we play one against the other.

One other thing about the above example. We could have put the television announcer's words in italics, but notice we didn't need to. New writers want to throw in italics all the time, but it slows and discourages reading.

There's one more way to handle back-story, and for this you will need italics.

Start each chapter with a short paragraph of history. Start the history at the beginning and work it along with the chapters, or do it in reverse, so that the climax arrives as the most pertinent bit of history is revealed. Readers will follow this if done with finesse. Trust their intelligence.

Flashbacks

When I mention flashbacks to people their eyes glaze over, like I'm talking Martian or Jupiterese. Flashbacks are nothing more than showing part of the story out of sequence. If we just want to convey a short bit of information or character background, we can inform our readers in interior monologue:

> Oself took a left at the next street and jogged down to the corner of Pine Road, stopping behind a light pole to catch his breath and stare down at his blue Lincoln.
>
> The car was two years old now.

> An impulse buy.
>
> More car than he needed, but it sure was comfortable to drive. Good looking inside and out, which is why he bought it. He needed a thing of beauty to replace the beauty that had been ripped out of his life.
>
> Except, as a substitute for his late wife, on a scale of one to ten, it turned out to be a minus eight million.

But if it is longer or we want to dramatize it, we can do it better in a flashback. The thing about flashbacks is to move in and out at some point:

> Oself stared out at new leaves on a scrawny tree rattling in the wind, sunlight saving it from being drab and grim. Sunlight. Sally's disposition had always been sunny, which had saved those stolen afternoons from being sordid and cheap.
>
> She bounced down the steps, caught herself and looked around, as if checking for anyone watching, then ran across the sidewalk and hopped in the front seat.
>
> "Where to this time, *mon cher*."
>
> He threw the car into gear. "You know I get horny when you talk French."
>
> "Mow de lawn, Chevrolet coupe."
>
> He had laughed as he headed for the Hideaway Motel at the end of town.

> He blinked as the sun flashed off the new spring leaves, stared at the scrawny tree a moment longer, then turned away.

If we analyze this we see the tree and new leaves and sunlight trigger a memory in the POV character. The first two sentences are in past tense, as is our story, but we lead into the flashback with the third sentence using past perfect "had been" and "had saved." Technically we should use past perfect for the whole flashback, "she had bounced down the steps," but this is clumsy to write and tiring to read, so once we lead into it, we continue in simple past tense. In the last sentence of the flashback we revert to the past perfect tense, "He had laughed," and then to simple past tense to bring us back into story-present. We also bounced back out of the flashback with the same tree and new leaves and sunlight, providing our readers the same entry and exit point to ground them in the main story, and also give them the feeling that no story-time has passed.

Okay, it's a jump from the tree to the memory, and the sun flashing off leaves, but I'm giving a down-and-dirty example of one way to do it.

Another way is to put the flashbacks in present tense:

> He didn't realize how precious their stolen moments were until it was over.
>
> She bounces down the staircase, stops at the cross hall, concern on her face for a moment, smiles, and runs to him. He takes her in his arms, kisses her, and they hurry out to the car. He drives to

> the motel and they yank off their clothes
> as they rush in the door.
> Now it was all gone and lived only
> in his memory.

The lead-in sentence is in past tense, then we slip into present tense for the flashback, and back out with past tense. I know this might seem contrary to use present tense for a story-past scene, but it works. Marcy Heidish does this well in *The Torching*. In a long scene, however, it might become tedious, depending upon the writer's skill.

Finally, a flashback can occur without fanfare at a chapter break, but the time difference should be established in the first few sentences. If story-present is at a hot summer beach, the flashback chapter could follow with a freezing snowstorm dreaming of next summer's beach vacation. Similarly, our POV character could be a bald man in a suit and in the next chapter he's a young man with a full head of hair and jeans. This works best if the end of one chapter hints at the time break in the next, such as POV staring in a mirror and wondering if there was ever a time he didn't shave, and the beginning of the next chapter starts with him staring at his peach-fuzz cheeks. We just have to make sure the switch is obvious or we'll confuse our readers.

I've heard of some writers advising never to use flashbacks, but this is like advising someone not to use a nail-puller when building a house. It's another tool in our workshop.

One of the best books I know for learning flashbacks is *Breakheart Hill* by Thomas H. Cook. He has flashbacks to being a witness in a trial, and then a flashback in the flashback to the event he's testifying about, then bounces back to the trial and finally back to story-present. And it all works. *Russia House* by John Le Carré is also good at manipulating time, as well as *Snow Falling on Cedars* by David Guterson, and *Cold Mountain* by

Charles Frazier. I recommend reading them to learn from their skill and techniques.

If we have an extensive back-story to reveal, it's always better to do it in flashback. This is almost as good as revealing something first hand in the main story. Following this, try dialogue and then, if it's short, interior monologue.

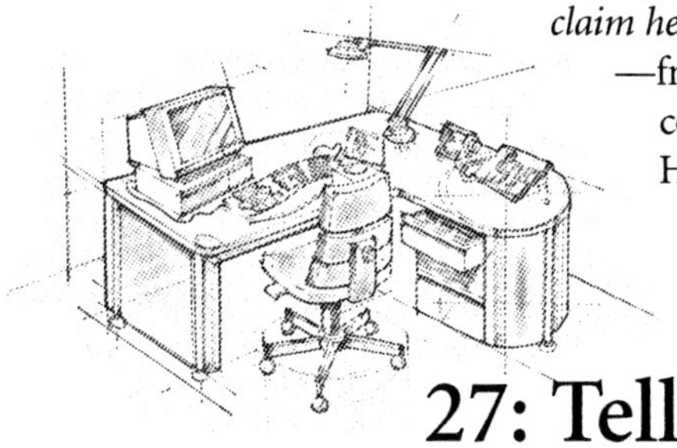

He might as well dip a pail in the ocean and claim he owned the sea.

—from "Paradise Lost," a story in the collection *The Mad Dog*, by Heinrich Boll

27: Tell Me What You Think

Critiques

If we can find a good critique group, other writers who will point out both pluses and minuses of our work, and offer constructive suggestions, we need to treat them like gold. I've known of a lot of writers who finally got published through the support and criticism of their critique group. The thing is in finding a good one. Too brutal a criticism too early in our careers can stifle creativity, while too gentle a critique in the later stages will not help us see the things that need correcting. And we need to know what is working as well as what is not. Many times it's just a matter of seeing things from another's perspective.

If we let someone read our work aloud, we hear it as a reader will read it rather than our own voice playing in our minds. I know of a critique group in Florida that has one reader. Everyone else comes in and anonymously places their work in a pile. I'm told that the one most critical is often the guy who wrote it, embarrassed of his own work.

If you join a group and your writing is critiqued, always thank them. Never argue. Never. It's okay to ask questions if something is unclear, but if you say, "what I was trying to say here was…" you need to go back and say what you were trying to say, not tell them what you were trying to say. And if we argue and criticize their critique, we could end up either alienating them or getting milquetoast comments. We have to be cool about this. They are not criticizing us, perhaps not even what we are saying, but the way we are saying it. If we cannot accept this objectively, we will never be able to profit from a critique.

Now, having said that, we shouldn't blindly accept everything either. A critique is another view of our work. We should seriously consider the recommendations and try out the suggestions, but in the end it is our work. The final judgement is always ours.

Writer's Workshops

I have less faith in writer's workshops. These are usually run by a teacher, probably a published writer, and the attendees present their work for critiquing. I think the difference is the paid teacher. He or she has a vested interest in putting everyone's work in the best light so those in the workshop will come back again.

In one workshop I was in, I mentioned that the format needed to be corrected if the writer hoped to submit it. The teacher replied that today, with computers, we can make our own format, which is grossly untrue. We'll talk about this in the chapter on format, but I've had too many agents tell me that when they receive something out of the norm, it tells them that the writer did not care enough to search out the proper format to present the work in a professional manner, which probably means the writing is not professional either.

But perhaps I'm being too harsh. This is my perspective from an experienced writer's viewpoint, and maybe the beginner will get a lot out of workshops. On the flip side of the highway, I heard that Tom Clancy gave a workshop once and when a student was discouraged about his writing, Clancy took the student out for coffee and spent an hour or two encouraging him.

So, remember what I said about this book being a naysayer. I'm just giving you my best cut, folks.

Classes

On the other hand, I've had a lot of success with classes. Marcie Heidish, who had seven books published at the time, and David Hoof, who had three, both taught at Georgetown University Extension School, and I learned a lot of good stuff from them. I would suggest you check out a local college extension course on fiction writing. We don't want an English teacher whose idea of creative writing is correct grammar. We want authors with credits to their names, people who actually have novels or short stories or poems in print.

I notice there are a lot of colleges offering Masters of Fine Arts in fiction writing, and Ph.Ds as well. I mean lots of them. And there are workshops and seminars all over the place. I sometimes wonder where all these writers are going to find a place to set up their computers. But there are a surprising number of people making a good living writing nonfiction, many of them freelance, for a zillion specialty publications handling medical journals, the auto industry, Capitol Hill lobbyists, and even a magazine for dry cleaners. Ha.

The thing is, while these programs will certainly give you the knowledge of what good writing is, they are no guarantee for fiction writers seeking publication. There is nothing that takes the place of sitting down and going through the grinding process of learning our craft. If in a query letter to an agent you mention that you have an MFA, it probably will give you an edge in getting them to look at your work, but in the end result, it's what's on the paper that counts.

Freelance Editors

Sometime in our writing we probably should consider hiring a professional freelance editor. The trouble is in finding a good one. Check out the warnings in our next chapter.

I've been lucky to have had two great ones. Marcy Heidish did an overall edit for me and David Hoof a line edit. I don't think I ever had anything worth reading before Marcy's, and both gave my writing a hundredfold jump in quality.

Overall edits will point out things that are generally wrong, such as writing loaded with clichés, filled with adjectives and adverbs, dialogue that all sounds alike. A line edit takes the manuscript line by line to show: passive sentences; payoffs that were not set up; redundancy; descriptions that worked and those that didn't; overwriting; and characters that don't cut it. It's more expensive, but you will learn much from it.

I thought at the time I knew all the things that should be avoided in writing, but when I actually had these things pointed out to me in my own work, it was a bombshell. Where did this stuff come from? What gremlin placed them there?

As a published author I have two readers, people I hold in high regard, before the manuscript gets to my editor who goes over it big time. Each one of them finds something. I think if I were a big name author, I'd hire a freelance editor every time. The thing is, it costs money to have a line edit and the writing income of most authors is below the poverty line. Which is why many authors are freelance editors.

At what stage of our writing are we candidates for hiring a freelance editor?

I'd like to say not until at least our second book. We learn so much writing the first one that almost any good reader or critique group can point out the flaws. But this is an individual thing and ya pays ya money and ya takes ya choice, as the old carny barkers used to say. If we've been at it awhile and need to take our writing up another step, and we have learned to accept criticism without treating it as a personal attack, go for it.

But never, never send them anything less than your best work. Why send them a first draft? Why pay someone to correct all the things you already know are wrong with it? As one freelance editor remarked, "I don't feel comfortable charging for mistakes I know can be self-corrected." All the freelance editors I've contacted only want to work with those who are serious about their writing.

If you hire one, expect to see a lot of blue ink. Or perhaps red. But that's what we're paying for, to show where we can improve our work. Hey, if you only want praise, don't use a freelance editor. Send me fifty bucks—don't even include the manuscript—and I'll praise it to the moon.

Treat a freelance editor as if you were sending a manuscript to an agent or publisher. We need to first look at chapter twenty-nine to make sure everything is in the proper format, lines double spaced, one inch margins around. If we are doing something wrong here, we need to know about that as well.

So, how much does it cost?

The quotes I've received from the freelance editors recommended to me were between $1.25 to $4.00 a page, but that range takes in vastly different services, from a line edit on the low end, to actually doing rewrites on the high side. Some will also do an overall edit, which will be reflected in the price. Also, some charge by the hour, so we really have to compare everything before making a decision. The charges should include some face-time or voice-time to go over the edit and answer any lingering questions.

The thing is, folks, I recommend we study the edit for at least a week before we contact our freelance editor. A line edit can be humbling. We want to make sure we've given ourselves enough time to both look at it objectively and to digest it fully. Only then will we be able to make full use of this consultation.

Still, there's one thing to remember. Just like we mentioned for critiques, the work is ours. It's our story. We make the final decisions on what to accept and what to change. But we're paying professional rates for all that blue ink, so we should not reject it lightly.

Is it worth it?

For me it was worth every penny and then some. I had a bunch of books under my belt at the time and was getting nowhere.

Okay, where do we find a freelance editor?

There are a lot of writer e-lists—e-mail exchanges—and writer bulletin boards on the Internet. I'd go out there and seek recommendations from other writers. Nothing is foolproof, but I think it's better than trying the magazine classifieds.

I've managed to collect the names of some freelance editors who were recommended to me to give you a place to start. They are from all over. It brought home to me how small the world has become when a writer in New Zealand recommended a freelance editor in Britain. Check them all out before you hire one. Make sure what services you are getting and how much you are paying. Know also that none of them, repeat, none of them will guarantee your manuscript will be publishable when it is over, but I think all of them would hope you'd come away with a better manuscript and a far better knowledge of the strengths and weaknesses of your writing and storytelling.

One last caveat. I have personally only used the services of David Hoof. And Marcy Heidish, whom I haven't been able to track down. What I'm saying here, folks, is that if one of these names doesn't work out for you, please don't take a picture of me picking my nose and publish it on the Web.

Nora Cavin, *noracav@cloud9.net*
Bobbie Christmas, *BZEBRA@aol.com*
Barbara DeMarco Barrett, *WritersOnWriting@aol.com*
Denise Dietz, *Calliope97@aol.com*
Audrey Dorsch, *exchange@ica.net*
Tracy Eastgate, *teastgate@home.com*
Jenny Hewitt, *jennyhewitt@cableinet.co.uk*
David L. Hoof, *d.hoof@worldnet.att.net*
Linda Wolfe Keister, *lwkeister@shirenet.com*
Margaret Searles, *mrsmillhark@juno.com*
Carrie M. Wood, *pclwood@mciworld.com*

Finally, two others asked to be included, one as a research source and the other as a nonfiction editor.

Ceceile Kay Richter, *crichter@ResearchSource.com*
The Research Source For Hard-to-Find Information

Ruth E. Thaler-Carter, *Rthalerc@aol.com*
Nonfiction editor

May we all end up on the best seller list. Me at the top. Ha.

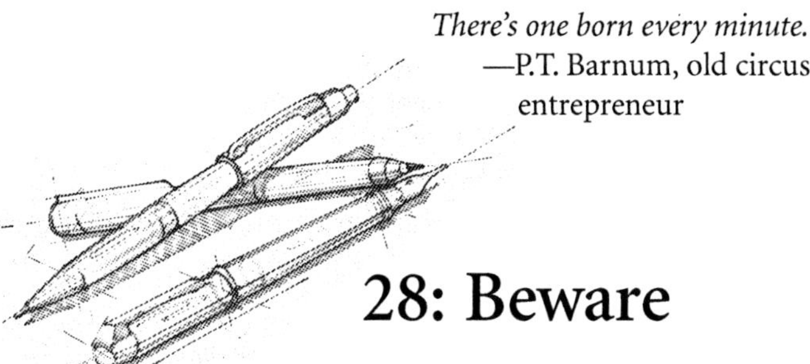

There's one born every minute.
—P.T. Barnum, old circus entrepreneur

28: Beware

Warnings

Of course, old P.T. Barnum, above, was talking about those who are about to be fleeced of their hard-earned cash.

Helloo-OO-oo, does that sound like us?

If we compare fiction writing to painting, at least an undiscovered artist can hang up his work for people to see, but a writer can't paste print on a wall and hope a visitor will go from page to page. Writers need readers. For that we need to be published. And for those of us who have been toiling away for weeks, months, years, this hunger for validation can build to the point where we can liken it to a hunger for cocaine or heroine. And just like there are dope dealers out there ready to take advantage of a craving for narcotics, so there are sharks out there waiting to prey on our hunger for publication. If we're not careful, we'll slip into a black hole.

Scams

There was a recent felony case brought against a New York editing company that charged big bucks for amateurish critiques. The way they got their clientele was through agents.

Say what?

When a writer submitted a manuscript to a less-than-scrupulous agent, sometimes even paying a reading fee, the agent would reply that the work would be publishable if it were edited by a professional and rewritten per their suggestions. Of course, they recommended the N.Y. Scam Company for the editing. If the writer didn't jump on that and contact the N.Y. Scam Company, the company would follow up with a letter to the writer, offering their services because the agent informed them the writer was an up-and-comer.

Who wouldn't be flattered by that?

The company charged thousands of dollars for which the agent got a good kickback, and the poor writer got empty pockets. Beware when an agent recommends an editing company.

There is also a pending case against a Southern agent that charged a hundred-dollar reading fee, which included a rudimentary critique. Sounds reasonable? Well, the critique always gave a glowing report with the probability the work would be published. The agent followed this up with a contract for his services, offering mouth-watering items that might come to pass, such as speaker's fees and television appearances.

After months of just trying to get someone to read our work, wouldn't our eyes bug out at this?

But, of course, we were required to put up four to five hundred dollars when we signed the contract, fees for duplication of manuscripts and mailings and reasonable office expenses.

How can someone be so gullible as to sign?

Well, don't forget about that hunger, and the glowing critique, and the probability our work would be published. There is also the huge temptation to earn back the hundred dollar reading fee we already invested by forking over another four hundred, but, then again, so is doubling-up on roulette.

But this agency wasn't finished.

After a few months went by, and not finding a publisher for our manuscript, they announced that they are investigating publishing a few highly selective manuscripts themselves. And a short time later, guess what? Our manuscript has been one of the selective chosen. If we will invest another four or five thousand dollars of our own money, we will not only have our book published, but instead of a royalty of ten percent we will be earning thirty percent.

Needless to say, no books were ever printed.

The scams have even gone high tech.

An on-line company offered, for a hefty monthly fee, to list my name and some of my work on their Web page where hungry agents came looking for new writers.

Hungry agents?

Looking for writers?

Two hundred or more query letters pass across an agent's desk every week, but the agent is still going out to check on this Web page? Oh, yeah.

We'll handle e-publishing in a separate chapter.

Vanity Presses

These presses prefer to be called subsidized or cooperative publishing. These are not really scams, doing what they say they will, but it's a matter of perception. They too will only take highly selective manuscripts. Read that as anyone willing to fork over up-front money. Quite a bit of money, but the come-on is that you will then earn four or five times more than normal royalties. They also talk of publicity and distribution, which mainly means you'll end up with a cellar full of books, but you'll have them to proudly hand out to your friends, which is why they're called vanity presses.

Sometimes writers latch onto a vanity press with the idea that once they have something in print, real publishers will take notice of them. The opposite is true in this case. Most agents and editors avoid vanity press writers like the plague. My recommendation, if you already have a few of these babies lurking in your cellar, don't tell.

Up-Front Money

Mainly let it be said: a reputable publisher will *not* charge you for publication. A reputable agent will *not* charge you a reading fee, will *not* recommend a high-priced company to edit your manuscript, will *not* charge you hundreds of dollars for up front expenses.

Reputable agents make their money through commissions on selling your writing. Reputable publishers make their money through book sales.

Up-front money is a scam.

I don't care what they call it, handling fee, reading fee, cooperative publishing, packaging fee; repeat after me, all up-front money is a scam.

Beware of those who promise the moon lest you end up holding a firefly.

Self-Publishing

But suppose we want to have something published anyway, even if we have to spend our own money? Say we want to print up a limited number of copies of a family journal, or some personal poetry?

Then self-publishing is the way to go.

Self-publishing is different than subsidized publishing. In self-publishing you control all the costs, how many books to print, what the cover will be like, and know up front you will be doing all the promotion yourself. You can self-publish a book cheaper than with a subsidized press, and it is not a negative with the publishing industry. I don't recommend it for fiction writers, but some people have done very well going this route. A writer I met from Texas lost his job and started self-publishing children's books, going around to the schools to promote them, got them into the Texas school system, which eventually let to a teddy-bear type doll of one of his characters. But unless you are a hustler, you'll end up with books in the cellar.

If you are thinking about self-publishing, you need to investigate what you are getting into. There are three books that deal extensively with this subject:

The Complete Guide to Self-Publishing, by Tom Ross and Marilyn Ross

The Self-Publishing Manual, by Dan Poynter

All-By-Yourself Self-Publishing, by David H. Li

I wish you well.

Writing Magazines

Futures, *Writer's Digest*, *Poets & Writers*, *The Writer*, *Writer's Journal*, to name a few, are certainly not scams. I read three of them and have a column in one. For a new writer there is always a wealth of information in them. For an established writer, there is always a new twist worth considering.

That said, there are things to beware of as well.

First, they all hype the success stories. Well, there is nothing wrong with that so long as we realize they are not the norm. It's only reasonable these magazines will splash success stories over their covers; they're in the business of selling magazines. We also have to realize that the hype is part of what makes a successful book a, well, a successful book. But for every one of those million-dollar auctions on a first novel, there are zillions out there not even getting looked at. And sometimes those million-dollar auctions turn out to be major flops and the author is never heard from again. I'd like to see one of these guys try to tempt me with a million bucks for a book I don't think is ready. Oh, yeah, I'd really like to see one try to tempt me with a million bucks.

The other thing we have to remember is that not all of the advertisers in these magazines have the care and nurturing of a new writer uppermost in their heart. As these magazines will attest. The idea, folks, is money. So all the warnings posted above apply. Be careful what you get into. Just because it is advertised in a reputable magazine doesn't mean it is a Consumer Report's Best Buy.

Conferences and Symposiums

There are many reader's conferences, such as Malice Domestic and Bouchercon for mystery readers, that a lot of writers attend to schlep their books. They usually have panels for authors to discuss topics of interest to the genre, plus a certain amount of how-to for those interested in making the jump from audience to author. They are great fun for authors and readers alike, but for the newcomer, they may be a little intimidating. There's a large crowd of people with everyone seeming to know one another because they've been coming to them for years, and the first-timer might tend to become the proverbial wallflower. I think most people are friendly and will take you into their circle if you make the effort. But I remember my first conference and so I'll tell you what I tell everyone: if you're feeling lonely and see me at a conference, come up and talk. I will be glad to introduce you to others I know. Especially if you've bought this book.

There are also hundreds of writer's conferences and symposiums around the country that deal from the writer's point of view, discussing many of the topics mentioned in this book, and often with agents on the premises to discuss what they are looking for in a manuscript with, perhaps, short agent interviews for individual writers to pitch their work. Washington Independent Writers Spring Conference has managed to do this for fiction and nonfiction writers.

My advice is to look at the writers headlining the conference and the subjects presented and go from there, but that doesn't always guarantee you will love the conference. Obviously, if my name is up there, it's got to be a great conference. Oh, yeah. At least for me.

The other thing to remember is that sometimes you may get just as much from a small, inexpensive conference as from those where you'll spend big bucks. If you're on the Internet, ask around for recommendations. On the other hand, if you want to spend the money to go to a conference in some exotic place, go for it. I think all the authors, agents, and editors at these conferences, big and small, are conscientious and will try their best to give the attendees their money's worth.

Writer's conferences are fun. We get to schmooze with other writers, share woes and joys, learn some new techniques, and perhaps make contact with an agent, but always remember that all the conferences and symposiums in the world will not help us develop our craft. Only sitting at the keyboard will do that.

One more thing about conferences and agents. It's always nice if you can talk to an agent at a conference and ask if you can send some sample chapters and an outline, but sometimes they are surrounded by aggressive people trying to do the same thing. The hunger for publication can make it seem like a feeding frenzy. Everyone desperate to make a contact that at the moment might seem like a matter of life and death.

So what happens if you are a bit timid and don't actually make contact, and don't get their blessing to send them three chapters and an outline?

Write them anyway and tell them they did. If they are freely dispensing this information, they realize it's a general offer to those at the conference, and with all those people crowding around, they're not going to actually remember everyone they met. And the end result is always the same; everything depends on the writing.

The message to take away from all this is writing is lonely and heartbreaking, full of mountain highs interspersed with soul-numbing lows. But if you have a burning zeal to string words together, do not be of faint heart. Hang in there in the knowledge that you have to do what you are doing, whether you ever get published or not, simply because you cannot *not* write.

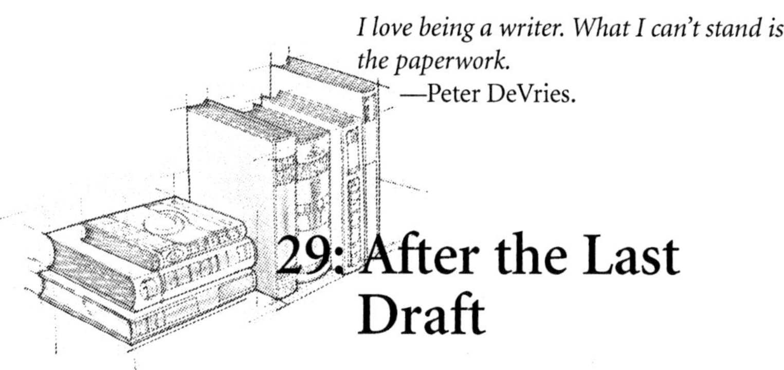

I love being a writer. What I can't stand is the paperwork.
—Peter DeVries.

29: After the Last Draft

Manuscript Mechanics

We've finished our last draft. Now what?

Now what is we take the time to make our manuscript as professional as possible. If you have a story worthy of the Pulitzer Prize, and you send it in handwritten on lined paper, or single spaced typewritten, or the wrong print font, there's a good chance it will never see the light of day.

You doubt my veracity?

Again?

Take a look at what literary agent Noah Lukeman says in the January/February 2000 issue of *Poets & Writers Magazine*:

> A simple thing like a manuscript looking brand new, but with maybe tiny folds in the corners, hardly noticeable, which might indicate the manuscript has been read before, will predispose the agent/editor against it.

He also talks about the other things we'll mention here, font, paper, spacing—anything that will make us look unprofessional. After all the work we've put into our novel, don't give them a reason to reject it because of format. Have I said this before? It is something we always have to remember: do not give them a reason to reject you.

Font:

Use Courier 10 cpi, 12 pt, which is Courier New, 12 pt on some word processors. Editors are used to this format, it's easy on their eyes, and it's what's expected. I used to use Roman 10 cpi, 12 pt, and I don't think it caused me any grief. But when I found out what the standard was, I bought a font module for my old 24-pin dot matrix Epson because I wanted to assure myself I was not getting less than an even shot at acceptance. The other reasons editors like Courier is that the placement of the letters makes it easier to insert a correction, and they can figure on two hundred and fifty words to the page. Use of any other fonts, in color, with doodads, or mixing fonts, will mark us as an amateur and get us treated as such.

Justification:

The manuscript should be left justified. Quite often word processors are set up for full justification, which gives two straight margins, one on either side, but in order to do this it spaces the words out unevenly. This translates into harder reading for editors' tired eyes. Left justified gives a straight left margin, but ragged right margin, with evenly spaced letters. I know, books are printed with full justification, but this is done only to save paper.

Paper:

Use white twenty-pound bond paper, eight-and-a-half by eleven inches. Once again, this is the standard. Why would we use anything else when it might tip us off as an amateur?

Printer:

If you have a dot matrix printer, it must be 24-pin letter quality. No editor is going to strain her eyes on 12-pin printing. And use a new ribbon for the same reason. This is not the time to go it on the cheap.

If you are using an ink-jet, watch the ink cartridge. We want clear, crisp printing that stands out and looks professional. And always print out a fresh manuscript for each submission. If you have a manuscript returned to you, don't be tempted to reuse it. Remember the quote from Noah Lukeman's article above. He also said to only use a laser printer, but from talks I've had with other agents, there seems to be no heavy bias against the 24-pin dot matrix or the ink-jet. However, I can't guarantee that, and since reading it I intend to use only my ink-jet for submissions.

Corrections:

No inked corrections. A computer is a blessing here. If some lines need changing, words misspelled, make the correction and reprint the page. If you are using a typewriter, the page has to be retyped. This not the time to be saving trees. If it eases your conscience, you can always cut up the discarded paper for notes or use the other side for drafts. If you find something in the manuscript that really doesn't make a difference, perhaps changing the order of the words in a sentence, but that you'd change if you had another chance, at least make the change on your hard drive. You may have to make another submission, or an editor may ask for some changes, and our preferred wording will be waiting.

SASE:

Always include a Self-Addressed Stamped Envelope. Always. Otherwise your manuscript may disappear into the ether. And include enough postage to return what you are sending. What I do when I send something out is to include only a #10 stamped envelop and ask the agent/editor to discard the enclosure upon completion. I'm not going to reuse the manuscript again, so why would I want to spend the extra postage to have it returned? This has become the norm for submissions.

Format

Title Page:

The title page should have your name, address, and phone number on the top left-hand corner. Your Social Security Number belongs here too, but with people stealing identities these days I leave it off until it's asked for. The word count goes on the top right. I always use the word count I get from my word processor, rounded to the nearest hundred. Centered on the same page, vertically and horizontally, is the title in caps on one line, followed by a double-spaced line—a single hard return with double-line spacing turned on—and "A NOVEL BY" and another double-spaced line to your name. If you use a pen name use that name and then under it in parentheses put your real name.

Subsequent Pages:

Title/Author's last name/chapter number on the top left-hand corner, and the page number on the top right-hand corner. If the title is long, FOURTEEN BIRDS SINGING IN A TREE, use one or two words of the title, BIRDS, or FOURTEEN BIRDS. Begin a new page for each chapter. All chapter numbers are centered between the margins and spelled out in upper case, like "ONE" with the first line of text one double line space below that. I start ONE halfway down the page with all subsequent chapters one-third down, but I think starting them all one-third down works.

Lines:

All lines are double-spaced, with no extra spacing between paragraphs. A break in scene or time in a chapter is signaled by a double-spaced line, three asterisks (* * *) and another double-spaced line. A dash break within a sentence (an em-dash) is signaled by two dashes--at the beginning and two dashes--at the end with no spaces on either side of the double dashes. Underline all text for <u>italics</u>. Do not italicize the words in the text. Underline is the standard format and it makes it easy for the typesetter to pick out and *italicize* it in the printed book.

Quotations:

For quotations within dialogue use single quotation marks. "I heard him say, 'He's no friend of Caesar,' to the governor."

Newspaper Articles:

The use of newspaper articles and television reports may change by editorial preference, but these are the preferences used by my editor.

Newspaper articles within the narrative are double indented:

> Calvin Goodknight, owner and head chef of "The Good Knight's Table," a regular on Baltimore's popular television show, "A Dash of Thyme," and a member of the technical board of directors of the Chef's Culinary College of Baltimore, died yesterday after ingesting poisonous mushrooms while lunching with friends aboard his houseboat, *Chivalry.*

Showing Reports:

Television reports are simply put into quotation marks as if the commentator were in the room talking, and then breaking for explanation of on-screen action. This is one of those instances when we want to tell, rather then show, what's happening.

Titles:

Titles are underlined: <u>The Baltimore Sun</u>; aboard the houseboat, <u>Chivalry</u>; Anne Lamott's book, <u>Bird by Bird</u>. Although sometimes editors want book titles all capped. Go figure.

General:

Make sure everything is polished and correct. Typos, spelling and grammatical errors can quickly get your work a jaundiced eye and perhaps even rejected. Agents and editors have little time to fool around correcting someone's manuscript, and if they see errors in the beginning they'll assume it will be that way throughout. Remember, don't give them a reason to turn you down.

There's only one way to succeed: accept failure as a temporary state, however long that state might be, and simply outlast it.
—Jim Cash, screenwriter, *Top Gun*

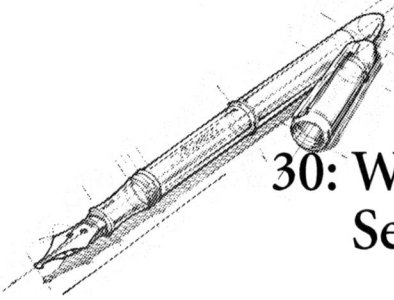

30: Where Do We Send It

Agents

Okay, folks, we've finally finished our novel, checked it over, made it is as polished and error free as we can, and put it in the right format.

What do we do now?

Here we have to decide if we are seeking a hard-copy publisher or one on-line. Since we'll take up electronic publishing in the next chapter, let's concentrate on hard-copy publishing for now.

So first, We look for an agent.

Why?

Because today's major publishing houses use agents as their first readers. Yes, we can send the manuscript directly to a publishing house, to Dear Editor, and in the old days occasionally such a book would be published, but these days our chances are just as good winning the lottery. If we send in a novel over the transom, as they say in the trade, it ends up in the slush pile where it will hibernate for months and may be returned without ever being read. And more and more major publishers flatly refuse to accept unagented manuscripts.

The reasoning is, if it's not good enough to be presented by an agent, then it's not good enough for them to spend their time reading it. And the agent, knowing this, will not present garbage to an editor because that can lead to the agent being dropped from the editor's reading list.

Make sense?

There is a small flaw in this reasoning. An agent may not submit an otherwise good novel if he doesn't think it will sell well. In today's market, most major publishers look down on books that will sell less than fifty thousand copies. It has become a bottom-line industry where most houses have been combined in conglomerates and want a capital return for their money somewhere between ten and twenty percent. So who gets dropped out? The new mid-list authors with sales of ten to twenty thousand copies. The flaw in this is that if they don't invest in new authors today, where will the bestsellers of tomorrow come from? I think their policies are shortsighted, but then, I'm prejudiced.

Why am I telling you all this? Because after you make the rounds of trying to get an agent, and you still have faith in your novel, there are the small presses and university presses and electronic presses to consider. For a new novelist, I think that's where the action is. But the sales are smaller, usually no advances, and a lot of agents will not submit to small presses.

Okay, if we want to try for the bigger bucks, the first step is to look for an agent. And as long as we're starting at the top, we might as well look for an agent either in New York or Los Angeles.

At one time these were the only agents to consider, but with e-mail and faxes and Web pages, this is no longer *de rigueur*. Also, while we are about it, we should be looking for an agent that belongs to the Association of Author's Representatives, AAR, who have an established code of ethics for their members. This is not proof that the agent is ethical, but it's a start.

Also, we do *not* want an agent that charges a reading fee, which AAR agents promise not to do. Remember that up front money is a scam.

Agent Charges

Agents make their money by charging a percentage of the sales, usually fifteen percent, higher for foreign sales. At first blush it might seem a good idea to pass on an agent and save that money, but I think this would be a false saving. As we have stated, they provide the entry to the big publishing houses and they know who is buying what. They will also shop a work around to see where they can come up with the best deal for their client. Which is us. Gotta remember, the more money they make for us, the more money they make for themselves.

They are also familiar with publishing contracts and will keep us from signing our lives away. This is especially true when it comes to dealing with the movie industry, which may sound like big thinking, but we never know what our writing will ignite. I'm sure we've all read about the sale of *The Bridges of Madison County* to the film industry. Because of the way the contract was written, the author received almost nothing from it. An agent would have prevented that. So in this case even paying ninety percent might have been worth it.

Good agents are worth every penny they earn.

Finding an Agent

So where do we find an agent?

There are four books that list them.

The *Literary Market Place*, LMP, lists just about everything there is in the publishing business. And just about every agent as well. You can buy one, which is rather expensive, or find it in the reference section at your local library. In it are listed the agent's name, address, genre, and what they want from a prospective client: query; three chapters; synopsis.

Guide to Literary Agents and *Writer's Market Place* go into more detail about agents as does the *Insider's Guide to Editors, Publishers and Literary Agents.* The last does not contain as an extensive a list, but goes into great detail on editors and agents and how to contact them.

There was also a Web page that has information about agents, www.agentresearch.com, at the time this book went into publication, but since the Net changes so swiftly I can't guarantee it is still in existence.

In searching for an agent, pay attention to the genre they are seeking. If we are writing mysteries, no sense querying an agent who handles only romances or nonfiction. We are not only wasting his/her time, but our own postage as well. And if the agent only wants a query letter, don't send him an eight hundred-page manuscript. Chances are you will not only waste his time, but lose his goodwill. And no agent wants to be phoned by someone he doesn't know, who takes up his valuable time, talking about something he doesn't care about. We can lose goodwill real fast there.

One more thing to remember here, nothing is hard and fast in this field. Everything is subjective. What works, works. But anytime we step out of the norm, we take a chance of alienating an agent from our project. If they ask for three chapters and a synopsis, guess what we send them? And if they ask for sample chapters, they mean the first three. If they only ask for a query letter, that's what I'd send, although we may get by enclosing the first three or four doubled spaced pages of manuscript. But always, whether with chapters or not, we include a query letter.

Query Letters

So now we are ready for the query letter. This document is as important as the manuscript. We will need it whether we are seeking an agent or a small press editor. If it is poorly written, chances are none of our manuscript will be read. I know, I know, you will say writing a good query doesn't mean you can write a good book, and vice versa, but this is the way agents and editors look at it, and it is their game. I've read statistics—don't hold me to this—that there are twenty thousand would-be writers for each agent. If this be true, guess who controls the chips? So make it the best damn letter you can, something worthy enough to go with your magnificent manuscript.

As we spent time making sure our manuscript was error free, we must do the same for our query. In spades. It should be written as a business letter, on quality paper, and with a heading if you have one. I buy a quality 20# paper for my queries, maybe off white or a light blue, something that sets it apart from ordinary paper. I want it to get quiet attention without putting them off. I also have a heading with a graphic logo that I made using one of the paint programs, but now I use a graphic of one of my published book covers. I wouldn't use a lot of different colors and fonts, but if you have a logo, you might use a splash of color there. We want to get attention, but we also want to come across as professional. For the main body of the letter, we use black Courier 12 pt or Courier New, the same as for our manuscript, what their eyes are used to.

The only purpose of the query letter is to get the agent or editor to take a glance at your manuscript. It is a sell letter. You probably have thirty seconds from the time it is picked up till it is discarded, so you better grab them in the first paragraph.

Pssst, your fly is open.

Recognize this from Opening Hooks?

This is the same idea we want to use for our query letter.

Of course, the best opening line is: "I have six books in publication with sales of twenty million." Now that baby will get immediate attention.

In lieu of that, we have to come up with a hook of our own, putting as much care into it as we have with the opening hook of our story. Seek the impact you want to make rather than being super-factual. For example, in a pre-published novel of mine, somewhere in the first chapter the heroine confronts the hero with a gun and nothing else. Instead of putting in some things that happened before, I tried right off for the most visual impact:

> When Marquis Judd meets Elfy Cane, she is standing stark naked, gun locked in her outstretched hands, pointing it dead center at his chest.

Bingo. That's the first paragraph. I wanted it to open the agent's eyes and drag them down to the next paragraph or, better, to look at the actual writing. In another pre-published novel I wrote, I took the general theme of the book and kedged it together with the book's name:

> *Ping Pong.* Bounced like a ball into a black and white dream so vivid he can taste it. *Ping Pong.* Now staggering around in an alcoholic daze at a funeral home. Was he going crazy? An old flame, now a psy-

chologist, thinks maybe he is. *Ping Pong.* And the world has changed again.

For *Bloody Bonsai* I tried to hook the agent with the novel's marketing possibilities and while it didn't get me an agent, it got me a publisher:

> The Elderhostel Catalog is distributed to a half-million affluent senior citizens at each printing. There are over one million bonsai enthusiasts in the United States. *Bloody Bonsai* is the first of the Elderhostel Mysteries.

Remember, we only have a few seconds to capture an agent's attention. Keep it short and to the point.

In the second paragraph we give them the genre and the length. Genre and word length are important because it tells them up front if it's something they can sell. If they have to guess, they might pass it by. We also might give them a two or three sentence synopsis.

> The *Eucharist Machine* is a fast paced mystery of 86,000 words. When Father Marcus Darby's woman friend is killed, he is the lead suspect, until he becomes the prime candidate for the next victim.

> *Bloody Bonsai* is a cozy mystery of 63,000 words. When widower James Dandy goes grumbling off to an Elderhostel, the last thing he expects the

> have is a good time, but that was before he meets a lovely widow and together they are charged with murder. It doesn't help that his new romance insists that they solve the case themselves. Then again, maybe it does.

In the third paragraph we mention our writing credits if we have any.

I read a query once where the writer mentioned she had been a member in good standing of Sisters-in-Crime for the past three years. My comment was, "Sorry, folks; while I'm a member of SIC and think a lot of it, I don't think that's going to impress an agent." But I have since learned from a couple of agents it might be something to put down. It might give her a little tick because it probably means she is at least familiar with the genre and some of the problems of promotion. An MFA degree might get a tick. I had a novelette published back in the midst of time and so I mentioned that and made big of the fact that it had sold a movie option, but I'm not sure it did a whole lot of good.

Of course if we've had some real published credits, put them down. We might even think about putting them up at the top of the letter.

I recently queried some new agents, and I had a small graphic of two of my book covers as part of the heading. I started right off with my credits, and this garnished immediate attention.

But if we have no credits, maybe tell them how long we've been writing, or just leave it blank.

In the last paragraph, tell them what you want, and thank them:

> I look forward to presenting sample chapters, or the entire manuscript, for your perusal in the hope you will be able to represent it. Thank you for your time and consideration.

This query uses a different approach; the letter is similar to one that I know got a lot of results. It could be used as a model for a synopsis as well.

> I have recently completed a 75,000-word thriller that I hope will interest you.
>
> *Always Leave Them Laughing* takes place within the confines of a small theater group in one of Long Island's more posh neighborhoods, during a production of *As You Like It.*
>
> Pompous and lecherous Reggie Van Clef is ecstatic when he is chosen as director for Sow's Ear Player's twenty-fifth anniversary production, which has some of the original cast members still active and eager to participate.
>
> All is going swimmingly until time comes to cast the production. Some of those original members are now leaders in the community, including one or two who well might be Mafia bosses. Suddenly Reggie is feeling the hot breath of shady characters breathing down his neck. And senior citizen women come climbing into his bed. Meanwhile, there's

> no end to the publicity, only increasing the pressure for choosing the cast.
>
> Reggie solves the problem by having so many stagehands they're coming out of the wings, and stand-ins for everybody. Only, some of the stand-ins become leads the hard way. Like when the bitchy ingenue ends up sleeping with the fishes.
>
> As it turns out, similar difficulties existed with Sow's Ear Player's original production during which the director disappeared under mysterious circumstances, never to be heard from again. This is enough for Reggie. He tries to slip silently away, but then he finds himself facing Mario the Enforcer who "don't want nobody skipping out before opening night." So Reggie's alternative is to come up with He-who-makes-people-disappear before he finds himself scuba diving without a scuba.
>
> *Always Leave Them Laughing* is reminiscent of Shelly Ogg's *The Round Tree Players* and might be similarly marketed. It is airy and humorous with romance, sex, and suddenly-dying people.
>
> I look forward to hearing from you and thank you for your consideration.

One other thing, if you met the agent, say at a conference or somewhere, or you have a reference from one of the agent's writers, I would use that up front and slip everything else down one paragraph.

Better yet, if you meet an editor at a conference or symposium and they invite you to send some chapters directly to them, follow everything we said about querying agents. If your work is accepted for publication, then go seek an agent, and see how easy it will be to find one. In this case I suggest you shop around, query Internet writer friends and ask their help and recommendations.

That's about it. My best skinny anyway. Just remember that if there were a perfect query letter model, everyone would be using it to the point of ad nauseam for agents/editors, so that anything different would then catch their eye and become the new model.

My advice is to take the example of the billboards.

Be quick, be short, be snappy.

And keep it to one page.

Small Presses

If we fail to find an agent, query the small presses and university presses in the same way we would an agent. Again, I think these presses are where it's at for the new mid-list writers. It probably means that we will not get an advance, and our distribution may not be as wide, but with today's Amazon.com and BarnesandNoble.com, the whole world has access anyway.

It will also mean we'll have to do all our own promotion, but that could be a blessing. I've met authors who have been picked up by the big houses and find that the house publicists are kids fresh out of college and are more hindrance than help. Also, the big houses ask your advice on very little, including the book's cover, the thing that will first attract a reader to our work. Often small presses will give us some input to everything, and my editors have been able to come up with some outstanding book covers.

Small Presses are listed in the *International Directory of Little Magazine and Small Presses*, Dustbooks, P.O. Box 100, Paradise, CA 95967, which you can probably find in your library, or they can order it for you. For university presses the Association of American University Presses publishes a directory annually that you may also be able to get from the library, or from the association at 71 West 23rd St., Suite 901, New York, NY 10010.

Rejections

I can guarantee we will be getting rejections. They always hurt. We send out a book with such promise and it comes back as unacceptable. That's a blow. But it's part of the learning process we have to go through to improve our craft. If we decide on our own we're good enough and just use a vanity press, we could end up never stretching ourselves to reach the next plateau. Rejections give us the incentive to improve.

Well, that sounds like bullshit, and maybe it is a bit. I've heard people tell me about good rejections, where an agent or editor wrote them a little personal note about their work. "You need to make your characters more real." "Great book, but not for me," is always a favorite. Whatever.

The thing is, folks, they may want to give you some encouragement because maybe they see some promise, but I wouldn't take them too literally. "Writing needs to be tighter." Well, maybe so, but they're just scribbling something that says the book didn't make it for them. Maybe because they have a book similar to ours already in the mill. So they say, "needs to be more vivid." And maybe so, but there's probably more things wrong with it than that simple scribbled note.

I guess what I'm trying to say is that you can take some encouragement from a personal note, but don't read more into it other than that.

So how do we handle rejections? Aside from tracking down the rejecter and helping him take a dive into wet concrete? As soon as we finish a book, we set about writing another, even as we're sending out the first. This has saved me because when the rejections did come, I was into the new book which gave me hope that even if the first one didn't make it, this great, fantastic one I was now working on surely would.

Finally, everything I've stated in this chapter could be negated by the next one on electronic publishing.

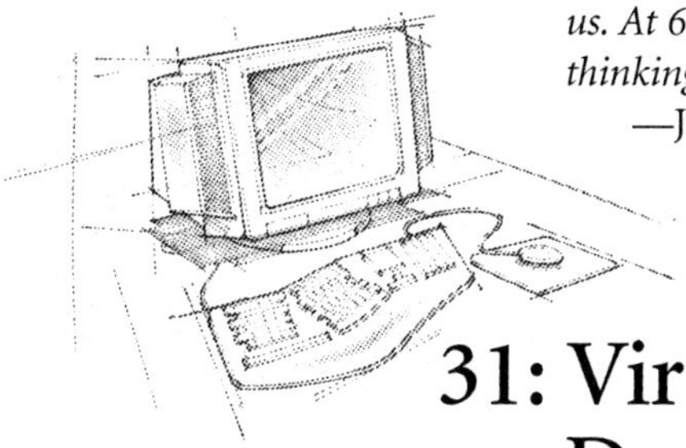

At age 20, we worry about what others think of us. At 40, we don't care what they think of us. At 60, we discover they haven't been thinking about us at all.
—Jack Falkson

31: Virtual and On-Demand Books

E-Publishing

We are on the cusp of an electronic publishing revolution. Maybe. Anything I say here is subject to change, and may already have changed by this time this book comes out in print. Change that "may" to "probably."

There are good electronic publishers out there who have been accepting quality books and trying to market them through three or four systems. First, they can be downloaded directly to your computer, if you feel like reading them on-screen, which few people do; but you can also print them out on your printer and read them as loose papers. The books can also be formatted for handheld devices such as the Palm Pilot and the Rocket eBook, the latter of which is about the size of a book and can hold a bunch of books in its storage. The people who use the latter say it's great. The format can be changed to a larger print, you can bookmark your place, and instead of carrying eight or ten classroom textbooks around, you only need this lightweight reader. Make sense? The problem is they have been priced around two to three hundred dollars. You can buy a lot of books for two hundred bucks.

Even so, I think there will be a lot of resistance to electronic books from older readers who like to hold a book in their hands, pass them around to friends, and see them on the shelves. But with more and more of the mellowing-into-fine-wine group hopping onto the Internet, maybe I'm wrong on this. Hard to tell with this swift-moving industry.

I think the younger generation who are used to seeing things on screen, like games and computers, will gobble them up.

The other thing about e-books is that writers like writing for them. They cut out the both agent and the big house publisher who has looked down on mid-list authors. They feel like it's their turn to thumb their nose. Also, the royalties are much higher, in the thirty- to fifty-percent range, and the books, not needing to be published on presses with expensive paper, are much cheaper. In the five- to seven-dollar range.

There is something else; the editors of electronic presses can afford to take a chance on something that might be a little iffy, cross genres such as a science fiction romance. Or they may take a chance on a writer that's borderline. These pioneers still reject a lot of books in trying to keep the quality of their houses intact, if you can call electronic publishers "houses." There are also big publishing houses getting into the e-publishing business now that the ground has been broken. The skinny is they plan to charge the same price for their e-books as their hard-press books and retain the same royalty for the author, but with the present-day e-publisher selling books in the five- to seven-dollar range, and giving the author thirty to fifty percent, why would a reader or author opt for one of the biggies?

Okay so far, but from here things get dicey.

The good news is that anyone, anyone can get published electronically.

The bad news is that anyone, anyone can get published electronically.

Some new electronic publishers, like iUniverse and Xlibris, with big publishing houses backing them up, will publish anybody. Xlibris has fees for various services, including copyright registration, what they call a homepage, and national accessibility. iUniverse, for their Writer's Club imprint, charges a fee right up front. Bottom line for either one is in the one to two hundred dollar range, and goes as high as $1,600. Then there are three or four others that are strictly on-line vanity presses.

These publishers hope to have twenty to thirty million authors on-line in the next ten to twenty years. Figure it out: at hundreds of dollars a pop, that is super big bucks. No wonder they are beneficently touting themselves as giving writers a way to present works unacceptable to hard-print publishers. But who will be the arbiter of quality? And without that, how does a reader browse through twenty million authors for a book he might want to read? One by one?

Does this mean all these pay-to-be-printed books will be worthless? No. But with thirty million authors on-line, how will the buying public know which are readable and which are not? Go through thirty million books and read their first chapters? Oh yeah, that works.

I can produce a book a week and have it published on a print-everybody electronic press. Will it be worth reading? I don't think so. Let me rephrase that. *No*. I'm talking about me here. I know my own writing and if I tried to write a book a week it would be pure crap.

Because of these print-everybody companies, I think this fledgling industry will take a big hit. Some readers will try out electronic books, get a few clunkers, and they'll desert in droves to go back to hard-print. If the hard-print publishers had deliberately set about trying to sabotage this new industry, I don't think they could have done a better job.

One of the bright rainbows everybody who is jumping on this bandwagon is touting: super-big-name Stephen King sold 600,000 copies of his e-book, *Riding the Bullet.* But according to an independent poll conducted by *The Book Report Network*, less than one percent claimed to have actually read it. Is it any wonder his subsequent offer was withdrawn after a few chapters?

My recommendation is, if you want to be published online, try one of the publishers who pay you to print your book, not one that you have to pay to print it. To quote my friend, Rex Anderson—*Cover Her with Roses, Night Calls*—"Publishers should pay authors. Authors shouldn't pay publishers."

So how would I feel about you if you did end up paying to have your book published by one of these print-everybody online presses?

I had ten or eleven books written before I had the first one published. I know the hunger to see our books in print. I don't recommend it, but I can surely understand it.

Print-on-Demand

I believe this will revolutionize the industry. POD, shorthand for Print-on-Demand, is already up and running, turning out trade paperbacks with some slick covers; but from the hard covers I've seen so far, it has a way to go.

POD allows a publisher to print any number of books, from one to a million, as the demand requires. This means there is no warehouse storage, no books to be remaindered, and no reason for a book to go out of print. Many of the electronic publishers are hooking up POD machines to get in the hard-print industry as well. There is even talk that some of the big bookstores will have POD machines on premises. Think of the transportation that will be saved. When a reader finds a book he/she wants, the store will print it out then and there. Talk about hot off the press.

But I wonder how the author will get paid.

Who will keep a record for us?

And will these big bookstores which are also a print-everybody on-line press, be pushing their own authors over the rest of us?

E-publishing and POD presents new problems for authors, but perhaps they'll be solutions as well. All I can tell you for sure is, changes are a-coming.

Three web-sites with information on e-publishing were up and running when this book went to press:

http://www.epublishingconnections.com/
http://www.ebookconnections.com/
http://www.ebooknet.com/

We have to keep up with this stuff because it's charging down on us like an eighteen wheeler.

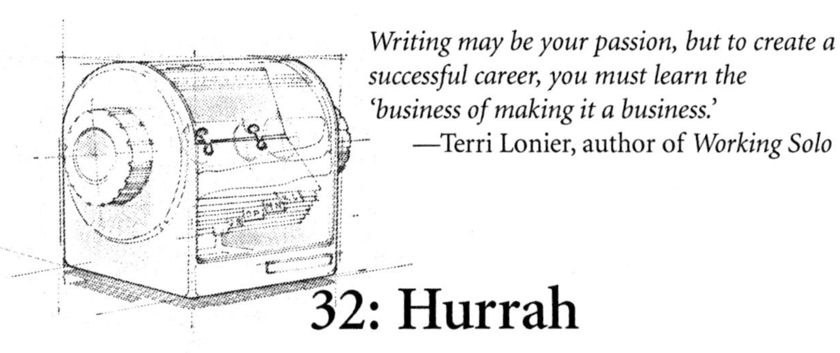

Writing may be your passion, but to create a successful career, you must learn the 'business of making it a business.'
—Terri Lonier, author of *Working Solo*

32: Hurrah

Acceptance

If we work hard, pray a lot, learn our craft, and have a tweak of luck, somewhere along the line we'll get a letter of acceptance.

Hoo rah.

We have just crossed a tremendous hurdle because it is my belief, no matter what the writing trade magazines say, not everybody will get published.

Good books and good writers can get passed over for a zillion reasons: the book is written at the wrong time, agents think the topic is overdone, or won't be of interest, or something just like it came out last week. The list is endless.

So our first job is to get published.

Oh, yeah, thanks a lot.

Like I didn't know that already.

What I mean is, aside from vanity and subsidized publishing, being published by any press opens a big door.

I think we all want to present our first novel to Super Agent who will auction it off and Super Big Publisher will buy it with a two million dollar advance. Do I dream of something so commercially crass for my magnificent writing?

You bet your sweet body parts.

Do I think it's going to happen?

In my dreams.

Editorial Review

When our book arrives at a publishing house, it will go through one or more initial readers. If an editor likes it, it goes to a review board where he/she will fight for it and where the decision about publication is made mostly on its moneymaking possibilities. In a small press the review might consist of the editor talking to him/herself in a mirror. Anyway, bingo, we make it to acceptance.

The book is ready to wrap up and go, right?

No, now's the time to make all the changes your editor will want.

My fiction editor, Dorrie O'Brien, came back to me so many times on my first book that I thought they never would publish it. I hated the changes she suggested, but thought I should at least try them and, surprise, they made the book better. There were a couple of things I held out against, and she let me have them, but on a first novel we don't have a lot of bargaining power. I was lucky. I have a good editor. The changes a friend of mine had to make did not improve her book.

My advice is to try the changes first, then pick out the battles you have to win, and keep them to a minimum. But it is still your book.

When we pass this stage, we'll get galleys—bound printouts—and we'll have a limited time to go though them and make corrections. Some things will slip by you, typos and subtle changes you editor slipped in. In looking over my books I found "he volunteered" and "he interjected" in places, speaker attributes I know I never used. Do your best to make them as error free as possible.

Then, somewhere nine months or more down line, we'll have the finished book in our hot little hands. I have known people to cry when they first gaze at it. Not a tough guy like me, a man, strong and bold, but others.

It's justifiable.

Publicity

When we finally get published, what do we do now?

Many pre-published writers think that once they finally have been published, yippee, they can now sit back secure in the knowledge that their career is finally underway.

This is the surest path to obscurity.

Now our main job it to get out and hustle as much as we can to make sure the first print-run is sold out.

To give you an example of the need to sell out the first edition, some years back my friend, mystery/thriller writer Beth Amos, was published in paperback by Harper, who sold some twenty-five thousand copies of her first book, maybe thirty-five thousand of her second, and sixty or seventy thousand of her third book, *but* none of them ever sold out the first printing. Harper didn't want to publish her books anymore under her real name. Forget that Beth had over a hundred thousand books out there, had built up a following under her real name, and never mind, folks, that she had pleaded with them not to have such a big print-run, she didn't sell out her first printing. Bottom line. Therefore, they will only publish her under a different name. When her agent queried other publishers, they looked at the same bottom line. They would publish her only under a pseudonym. This is one of the reasons authors are published under more than one name.

It is or was an axiom for college professors to publish or perish. For writers it's publish and publicize or perish.

So how do we do that?

There are a lot of good books on publicity for writers, suggesting ways to get on television and radio stations and book signings and on and on. When you first get word that your writing has been accepted, I suggest you celebrate by going out and buying one. Three I know of: *Jump Start Your Book Sales*, by Marilyn and Tom Ross; *The Complete Guide to Book Publicity*, by Jodee Blanco; *1001 Ways to Market Your Books*, by John Kremer. When I looked over these books, I flipped through them and bought the Ross book first. Only later did it occur to me that I did so because of the white space and easy format. See what I meant about white space back in chapter ten?

I can tell you what I do, but I'm not a good publicist. My goal in life is to make enough money writing to hire a professional publicist so I don't have to do it myself, but in order to do that I have to first publicize my book so that I can make enough money writing to hire a professional publicist. Ugh.

The first thing I do when a book is coming out, I call all the bookstores and try to set up a reading and/or a signing. Big bookstores are not always interested. The smaller bookstores have been more generous to me. But for me book signings have been a mixed bag. I'll do them at the drop of a hat, wherever and whenever I can, but I remember driving sixty miles one dark and stormy night to a big bookstore to talk to one person who had left his wallet at home—still, I treated him like he was fifty people rolled into one. I ended up at a bookstore once just to talk to the storeowners, but at least I knew they would try to push my books. But I don't have an aggressive sales personality.

My friend, Marcia Talley—*Sing It To Her Bones*—can practically accost people passing by in a mall and talk them into buying her book. And she has sold a passel of books touring the country wherever she has relatives and friends to put her up. If you can do that, great.

So you have to figure out what works for you.

What I do is spend more time trying to get people to review my books. Even a bad review is good for me, because that at least keeps both me and the book before the public.

I'll give a speech at the drop of a hat and actively seek engagements, bringing along my books, of course. I actively seek interviews, make contacts through writer's organizations such as Sisters in Crime, and attend conferences where mystery readers gather, such as Bouchercon and Malice Domestic. Do I sell a lot of books there? Not so much it pays my way, but it keeps building.

I think what I have done more than anything is to reach out to people on the Internet. I have put out a series of fiction technique hints on my Web page and on some bulletin boards, which gets my name out there and, incidentally, led to the contract to write this book. Since my books right now are Elderhostel Mysteries, I've even gone one-on-one with e-mails to people who go on Elderhostels, telling them about my book and asking them to tell others.

In spite of how lightly I'm taking this here, I really urge you to buy a couple of books on publicizing your novel when the time comes, because publicity really is the name of the game.

And I'm going to do a lot more myself, just as soon as I hire my professional publicist.

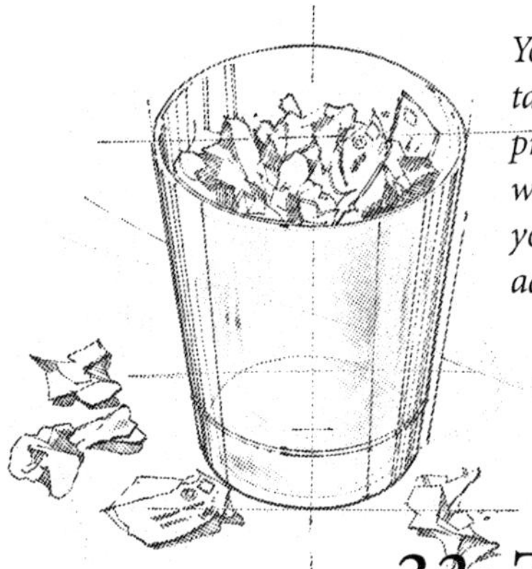

You must want to do it enough. Enough to take all the rejections, enough to pay the price of disappointment and discouragement while you are learning. Like any other artist you must learn your craft—then you can add all the genius you like.

—Phyllis A. Whitney

33: This Is It—There Ain't No More

There's probably more I should say about writing, but the book has to end sometime. Which if you get into the business of rewriting you'll find that sometime you have to say, that's it. It's finished. We can't keep rewriting the same book for the rest of our lives.

And finishing a book might sometimes be depressing. We've been traveling with these characters for months, maybe years, become comfortable with them, shared our life with them, and now they are leaving us. Our best friend just moved cross-country. What's facing us is a lonely journey into an unknown land. Yes, it's also filled with fresh opportunities and adventures, but it's hard to see that when we've just stepped off our old familiar path into a fields of dandelions.

Thing to remember is, it takes a certain amount of courage to write a novel. The first day we sit down to face a lined legal pad, or a blank paper in a typewriter, or a clear computer monitor, and we start stringing words together, everything is new and unknown. We're setting out on a road we know we'll be traveling on for nine months to a year, maybe more, without any assurance we'll find a pot of gold at the end of the trail. Or even that we'll find the end of the trail. That takes courage. Or sheer stupidity. In my case, I think it's the latter.

Each time I start a new book I wonder if I'll be able to finish it. If the pieces will come together. If the story will be worth reading. If the characters will come alive. Or if I'm just kidding myself.

Each book we complete gives us hope for the next. We've climbed that hill. It doesn't get easier, but knowing we made it before helps in trudging up the slope once more.

This is a noble craft we are undertaking.

Writing is man's greatest invention.

In the August 1999 issue of the *National Geographic Magazine*, Joel Swerdlow, in an article on "The Power of Writing," states that civilizations are dated from the time they start writing. It is only after they put things down in stone, on papyrus and parchment and paper, that we can know the details of their lives—history, beliefs, names and dates, thoughts, technology, accounts, emotions—that we come to know their stories.

In 1999, PBS had a program that went back over all the inventions of the past millennium to decide which had been the most important. Winning hands down was Gutenberg's printing press in the middle of the fifteenth century. For the first time, books could be mass-produced and put into the hands of ordinary citizens. The printed word had an almost magical power. Words written on paper, created by ordinary citizens, have overthrown governments and changed the course of history.

"When in the course of human events..."

Think of all the different dishes and foods we've eaten because we can buy a book of recipes. Without writing, our technology would still be in the stone age.

Do we realize that it wasn't until the seventh century that it became standard practice in Western culture to put spaces between words? Hoo boy. Imagine how that would have played on our computer's spell checker.

I think stories probably spurred the invention of language, and good stories, ones we wanted to keep around, probably spurred the invention of writing. An ancient king gained immortality by bards telling of his great adventures, and the written word gave it permanence.

We are the inheritors of those old tellers-of-tales who gathered people around in drafty old castles and beside campfires in the desert, to weave words into great epics, yarns to amuse and entertain, fables to teach great proverbs.

Christ himself taught in stories for He knew it was the most powerful form of learning.

So now it is up to us to pick up that mantle and carry it forward. Unlike the bards of old whose words only affected those within the sound of their voice, thanks to Gutenberg, and the World-Wide Web, someone in a faraway land can take our string of words home on a cold winter's evening, sit in front of a fire with a hot cup of soup, and be transported into another world. Words to entertain, to amuse, to teach. The ancient and honorable craft of storytelling.

It's one thing to know what good writing is; it's another to put it into practice. Yet I believe it is our sacred duty to give our readers the best possible words we can.

In the Elizabeth Barrett Browning poem "Aurora Leigh" is a passage regarding Moses' encounter with God in the burning bush that I think is hilarious, and no one else seems to:

> Earth's crammed with heaven,
> And every common bush afire with God;
> But only he who sees takes off his shoes;
> The rest sit round it and pluck blackber-
> ries.

We, you and I, must strive to write so that we have to take off our shoes.

If you find in my books that I have not followed all the things I've mentioned here, about easy reading writing, know that it's not for lack of trying, but because easy reading is damn hard writing.

9 781893 818057